ERIC GILL: WORKMAN

He who praises a man ought to follow him, and if he be not ready to follow him he ought not to praise him.

—*St. John Chrysostom.*

MODERN CHRISTIAN REVOLUTIONARIES

ERIC GILL: WORKMAN

By

DONALD ATTWATER

We may recover something of our lost equanimity, our lost integrity, our lost innocence when, instead of seeing things as things to be grasped and possessed, we see them as beings manifesting Being himself.—*Eric Gill.*

WIPF & STOCK · Eugene, Oregon

Wipf and Stock Publishers
199 W 8th Ave, Suite 3
Eugene, OR 97401

Eric Gill
Workman
By Attwater, Donald

ISBN 13: 978-1-5326-8477-7
Publication date 3/13/2019
Previously published by James Clarke & Co., LTD., 1941

To

MARY ETHEL GILL

PREFACE

THE writing of this short book has been a task of very considerable difficulty, for intrinsic as well as extrinsic reasons. My aim has been no more than to give a summary exposition of Eric Gill's ideas and the convictions that lay behind them, primarily with the object of encouraging my readers to turn to Gill's own writings and study them for themselves. But to expound Gill is very difficult, because he is already expounded extraordinarily well and clearly in his own works, whether written or other. The *Autobiography*, in particular—to read it is to hear Gill talking, answering our objections, joking and chuckling, gently touching out our sillinesses; therein he is no longer putting forth his ideas as it were for our enlightenment: rather are we shown how these convictions came to force themselves upon him, not simply by a process of ratiocination from abstract premises, but by the total various activities and experiences of a full life. "Who touches this book, touches a man"—the tag comes true.

He called it "a record of mental experience", and so the prospective reader might make the mistake of supposing it to be a "highbrow" work, with a lot of talk about the soul, lofty abstractions and philosophical terms, and no getting down to the brass tacks of daily life. Not at all. "I preface this book", he wrote, "with the statement that man is matter and spirit, really both, conjoined and inseparable. The record will be concerned with the spiritual as informing the material and with the material as manifesting the spiritual." On the title-page are printed the words *Quod ore sumpsimus*. . . . For the Catholic these words have a specific reference to the sacramental body and blood of Christ, but they may be taken in a more general sense. "What we have taken with our mouth", that is, all bodily, sensual experience, *pura mente capiamus*, "may we receive with a whole mind." Biographically we are enabled to see that that prayer was fulfilled: Eric Gill was a man of whole mind.

I therefore have scarcely done more than string together a succession of quotations and paraphrases of Gill's own words—and I gratefully acknowledge the generosity of his various publishers (*see* the bibliography which follows) in allowing me to take these liberties with their publications. It was my privilege to know Eric intimately for eighteen years, and I necessarily read his books in the light of that happy experience; I sincerely hope I have nowhere distorted his meaning and nowhere made obscure what he made plain: I am an ordinary man, writing about another "ordinary man", and this book is intended for other ordinary men and women. Of them I would ask only one thing over and above their good will: Please read this book, and still more Gill's own books, with a free and open mind; as Bacon said of studies in general, we should not read to contradict and to confute; it does not matter if we do not agree with all we read: what matters first is that we should get a vision of this good and great man, whose ordinariness was part of his greatness.

I hope I shall not be accused of the partiality of a friend when I declare my conviction that Eric Gill was one of the few great men known to our time: not simply great at this or that, but a great *man*. But I have attempted no portrait of him; it is not possible: as Gilbert Chesterton wrote of his dead brother, "As a friend he is too near me, and as a hero too far away."

D.A.

In the night of
November 17-18, 1941

BOOKS BY ERIC GILL

Art Nonsense. Twenty-four essays. Cassell, 1929.
(Quotations herein are from the pocket edition, 1934.)

Clothes. Cape, 1931.

Beauty Looks After Herself. Thirteen essays. Sheed & Ward, 1933.
(Quoted herein as *Beauty.*)

Unemployment. An essay. Faber & Faber, 1933.

Money and Morals. Three essays. Faber & Faber, 1934.
(Quoted herein as *M. & M.*)

Art and a Changing Civilization. (In the Twentieth-Century Library.) Lane, 1934.
(Quoted herein as *Art.*)

Work and Leisure. Three essays. Faber & Faber, 1935.
(Quoted herein as *W. & L.*)

The Necessity of Belief. "An enquiry into the nature of human certainty, the causes of scepticism and the grounds of morality, and a justification of the doctrine that the end is the beginning." Faber & Faber, 1935.
(Quoted herein as *Belief.*)

Work and Property. Eight essays. Dent, 1937.
(Quoted herein as *W. & P.*)

And Who Wants Peace? (Pax Pamphlet No. 1.) James Clarke, 1938.
(Quoted herein as *Peace.*)

Social Justice and the Stations of the Cross. James Clarke, 1939.
(Quoted herein as *Stations.*)

Sacred and Secular. Six essays. Dent, 1940.
(Quoted herein as *S. & S.*)

Christianity and the Machine Age. (Christian News-Letter Books, No. 6.) The Sheldon Press, 1940.

(Quoted herein as *Machine Age.* This is an excellent summary, in seventy pages or so, of Eric Gill's beliefs and teaching.)

Autobiography. Cape, 1940.

(Quoted herein as *Auto.*)

Last Essays. Nine essays, Cape, 1942. This was published too late to be made use of in the present book. The essay called Education for What? is outstanding.

A detailed bibliography of the writings of Eric Gill is being prepared by Evan R. Gill.

1

ARTHUR Eric Rowton Gill was born on February 22nd, 1882, at Brighton, and his first home was in a suburban street of this town which he afterwards characterized as a shapeless and meaningless mess. He was the second of thirteen children. His father was a minister of that small sect, "connection", called after its foundress, Selina, Countess of Huntingdon, and he was a man of earnestness, culture and probity, of a type very common in nineteenth-century England. Eric had other ecclesiastical associations: not only did he marry the daughter of the sacristan of Chichester cathedral, but his paternal grandfather and great-uncle were missionaries in the South Seas, as were two of his brothers and one sister. When the present writer first knew him, after the war of 1914-18, he would often disclaim any missionary enterprise for his own convictions, but as the years passed he became in fact more and more of a missionary, "publicist", and would sometimes with a wry smile refer to his family tradition in playful extenuation.

But this was not the only, or the most important, thing concerning which early influences persisted. Unlike so many "rebels" from the English middle and professional class, Eric Gill never (except possibly for a brief period in his youth) deliberately cut himself off from his origins; particularly did he never foul the nest of his own family and upbringing. I have said that his father was a typical Victorian, and it has been acutely noted by David Jones that Eric himself was, in a way, a Victorian person—not least in his solid sincerity and high seriousness, combined with a gay frolicsomeness such as is found in the mathematician Dodgson or in Lear (Edward, not the Shakespearian king). The Gill household was a happy one, and it was poor, really poor, from the point of view of ways and means; so far was this from having an embittering effect on Eric (or, I believe, on any of them) that it was the practical starting-point of his own repudiation of worldly wealth and his attachment to a decent poverty as a fundamental necessity for any good revolution, personal or social. It was a cultured family—the father had some skill as a painter, the mother as a singer, and a glance at their children's names shows their literary interests (Eric, "or Little by Little", Kingsley, Carlyle, Maurice, MacDonald, Robertson, Enid from Tennyson). But above all it was a religious family: "We took religion for granted just as we took the roof over our heads. . . . But taking things for granted doesn't mean you aren't interested in them or that, on occasion, you won't be very interested indeed" (*Auto.*, p. 59). And the religion was that combination of evangelical doctrine and upright conduct, combined both with strict domestic discipline and dissenting independence, that at its best has been so valuable a factor in making the modern English character: the "nonconformist conscience" is despicable only in its decay. The young Gills were brought up on virtuous principles, and "these principles were put before us in such a way as to win our assent to them—assent both notional and affective" (*Auto.*, p. 56).

Eric's schooling lasted some half-dozen years, in a private school at Brighton, and consisted solely of "learning things out of little books and being able to remember enough to answer questions". It made no particular impression on him, and he showed no special aptitude for book-learning: his real enthusiasms were cricket and football, not as competitive contests but as things worth doing for their own sake—games, and drawing locomotive engines. In later life he made no complaints against the sort of teaching he had received: rather was he thankful that his schoolmasters had been too timid or too uninterested to try to coerce his mind or to mould him against his proper nature. Naturally he came to have ideas on schooling: these he never had the opportunity to work out and develop (though he used them with startlingly good effect in bringing up his own family), but their foundation was that children should be given a good comprehensive view of the world in general, showing the growth and decay of peoples and nations in the light of man's spiritual nature and eternal destiny; and that the amount of formal learning to be done should be kept down to the lowest possible minimum, for we are educated, not by learning, but by *doing*—"that is, in my mind, the whole secret of education, whether in schools or in workshops or in life". He did not think it really matters much whether a person can read and write, and it seemed to him unreasonable "to burden the budding mind of a child with too much high intellectual stuff" about duty and culture and all that sort of thing. Mathematics was the school subject that most appealed to him: it called for that accuracy and precision that had already been inculcated at home, it ministered to an appetite for orderliness that was to increase with his years. The *Autobiography* gives a strong impression that the young Eric was an intelligent, observant, sensitive boy, in no way "freakish", healthy in mind and body, whose favourite author was G. A. Henty.

"The children of large families, especially when the parents are poor, do not complain with bitterness because they go short of clothes, firing or food. Unless their minds are poisoned by jealousy or covetousness, they regard all such hardships as being part of the game of life, and, as is well known, no people are happier than the children of the large families of poor parents when those parents are engaged in humane occupations, even under hard conditions, provided that the parents are examples of justice and charity" (*Belief*, p. 222).

When he wrote those lines Eric Gill certainly had his own early home in mind. "The shepherd boy who helps his father in the cold nights of the lambing season does not curse the physical universe and refuse to attend church or chapel on Sunday." During the past couple of generations many comfortably-circumstanced (and other) people have refused to attend church or chapel—"abandoning institutional religion" it is called—for various reasons, often cogent, often not; parallel with this phenomenon has been another, much smaller, less picturesque and fashionable and therefore less talked about, of people abandoning unbelief or an elastic undogmatic form of religion for one more vigorous, exacting and authoritative, in other words, seeking for a teaching church. When Eric Gill became a Roman Catholic in 1913 he went on from where his father had left off. Mr. Gill senior had resigned from the Congregationalists because he, the shepherd, would not have his religious message dictated to him by his flock; the Countess of Huntingdon's Connection received its doctrine "from above" ("which is the proper place for doctrine to come from"), embodied in the Anglican Book of Common Prayer; then, in 1897, he took the next step in the same direction and joined the Church of England, taking his family with him. This was an important date in his eldest son's life, not simply because Eric was taken away from school, at the age of fifteen, but because they all went to live at Chichester, and the effect of this city on the growing boy's mind was profound. Not because it was old (which it is) or "picturesque" (which it isn't) but because it was an ordered human thing: not a disorderly mess made by the speculative builder, like the Brighton suburb, but "a place, the product of reason and love. . . . Here was no dead product of mathematical calculation, no merely sanitary and convenient arrangement. Here was something as human as home and as lovely as Heaven. That was how it seemed to me. . . ." (*Auto.*, p. 77). For a time he studied drawing and lettering at the local art-school, but got considerably more out of his own drawing and exploration in the cathedral and from the wise friendship of one of its prebendaries, Doctor Robert Codrington. It was a time compounded of "rapture and rebellion"; the mental and physical surge of adolescence was disturbing him. So he became dissatisfied and unhappy, and after two years he was sent off to London to be apprenticed in the large drawing-office of an ecclesiastical architect.

The first three of the next five years was a period of disillusionment, disintegration and revolt, first against religious mugwumpery, then against social and political perversions, lastly against the fatuity and play-acting that passed for architecture. Eric Gill began to be interested in "revolution". "Religion in St. Saviour's, Clapham, and irreligion in the architect's office were unequally matched. Nothing in the outward show of that Christianity could possibly hold me—the frightful church, the frightful music, the apparently empty conventionality of the congregation. And nothing that the parson ever said seemed to imply any realization that the Church of England was in any way responsible for the intellectual and moral and physical state of London" (*Auto.*, p. 108). So he slid out of Anglicanism into a vague and hungry agnosticism, and seeing that most professional politics was as much a sham as a great deal of professional religion, that Parliament did not represent the people and laws were really made in board-rooms and private gatherings, he became in an equally nebulous way a socialist. But he kept his head. Youthful "emancipation" not seldom dissolves into licence, liberty is made a cloak for malice: young Gill did not take that easy path, if only, as he modestly implies, it did not look all that easy to him. As for architecture—and here too he owed much to the sensitive conscience and clear mind of a fellow draughtsman, George Carter—he soon saw that it was not the same thing as building and that the tyranny of the architect in his office had reduced the working mason and builder to the mere copying of things designed on paper in the smallest detail by other people. Such irrational and inhuman division of labour was not for him: he wanted to be a workman, with a workman's rights and duties, to design what was to be made and make what he had designed. What work that he could do was wanted? He soon found it—letter-cutting in stone. In the evenings he went to the writing-classes of that great man Edward Johnston; after twelve months he got his first small commission, and from that day forth was never out of a job. He just walked out of the architect's office.

In 1904, at the age of twenty-two, Eric Gill married, and set up house in a block of workmen's dwellings in Battersea. Before very long, after the birth of two daughters, they removed to Ditchling in their native county. There was no "back-to-the-land" sentiment behind this, though Eric always loved the life of the earth—and especially "the earth that man has loved, for his daily work and the pathos of his plight"—and Mary his wife was a farmwife by second nature. What was behind it was the conviction from experience that a big city was no place in which to bring up children. " . . . we were not only able to marry young . . . but also . . . I was subjected to the influence of marriage without the complications of suburban snobbery and domestic indignity. . . . Marriage meant babies—if it weren't for babies there wouldn't be marriage. . . . But the consequences are momentous. You are no longer simply concerned to discover what conditions are best for your work (that which you do for your living—*i.e.*, in return for the bread and butter you eat) and what conditions are best for your comfort, you are concerned to discover what conditions are best for a growing family" (*Auto*., pp. 132-34).

Meanwhile the inscription-cutting and tombstone business was prospering, and Gill's skill brought him to the notice of such as Roger Fry and found him a friend and customer in Count Kessler, of Weimar. In 1909, with much diffidence and trepidation, he made his first essay in stone-carving, a female figure, and this new venture at once drew more attention to him. Sculptors nowadays mostly *model* their statuary, building it up in clay, and then have this model reproduced in stone by a professional carver with various machines and gadgets: here was a man who carved his thing himself directly out of the stone; one, moreover, who thought in terms of stone (not of clay) and of carving (not of modelling). 'So all without knowing it I was making a little revolution. I was reuniting what should never have been separated: the artist as man of imagination and the artist as workman . . . I really was like the child who said 'first I think and then I draw my think'—in contrast with the art-student who must say, 'first I look and then I draw my look'. Of course the art critics didn't believe it. How could they? They thought I was putting up a stunt—being archaic on purpose. Whereas the real and complete truth was that I was completely ignorant of all their art stuff and was childishly doing my utmost to copy accurately in stone what I saw in my head. . . ." (*Auto.*, p. 162). Despite this misunderstanding the "art world" opened its doors to receive him; Epstein and John, Ambrose McEvoy and William Rothenstein were among his friends; he was "given the opportunity to become acquainted at close quarters with the leading intellectual and artistic folk of our great empire"—and then, not for the first or last time, Gill saw himself standing at the edge of a yawning pit of danger, and drew back: or rather, not scorning the tactics of the Desert Fathers or St Benedict, he ran away, "escaped".

> Among the artists "there was no smell of burning boats—burning boats was the one thing no fellow should do. I think it might not unfairly be said that they all believed in beauty, were interested in truth and had doubts about the good. . . . I was so very much not the artist as they were artists, and though I was an agnostic in those days I was so very much not the sceptic as they were sceptics. . . . They most certainly believed in something called Art and I most certainly did not, and I came more and more to detest the whole art world. I believed in religion and was desperately trying to find it, and they seemed to regard religion as being essentially nonsense but valuable as a spur to aesthetic experience and activity. . . . I say I did not believe in Art or the art world. But of course I believed very much in the arts—with a small a and an s—whether it be the art of cooking or that of painting portraits or church pictures. But that's a very different matter and puts the 'artist' under the obligation of knowing *what* he is making and *why*. It ranks him with the world of workmen doing useful jobs. And as for the art *world*, well, that is even more sickening, especially when all the snobbery of

intellectual distinction comes in. . . . Everybody was extremely kind and refined—and distinguished, but 'I'd rather be a heathen suckled in a creed outworn. . . .' On the other hand, in yet another sense, I believed in art very much indeed. The artist as prophet and seer, the artist as priest—art as man's act of collaboration with God in creating, art as *ritual*—these things I believed very earnestly. But here again I was generally at variance with my high-art friends. Their views were both more simple and more mysterious than mine. They were essentially aesthetes: that was the awful truth. They played about with religion and philosophy and labour politics, but that was all very superficial; what they really believed in and worked for was aesthetic emotion as understood by the art critics. But art as the ritual expression of religion I did indeed believe in and they did not. . . . So I gradually escaped from the high-art world which for a time seemed to be closing round me. Doubtless I never was a serious artist as serious art was understood in that world. I was the son of a nonconformist parson, the grandson of a missionary. Life was more than art" (*Auto.*, pp. 172-74).

The last two sentences are among the most significant pieces of self-revelation in all Gill's *Autobiography*. But before that repudiation could be complete, before he could become a citizen of a new and whole world, another and final crisis—"the end is the beginning"—had to be passed.

§

Gill was in process of solving—*solvitur ambulando*—the problem of work; but he was also faced with the problem of social injustice, and that depended on religion. There was the evil of having too little material goods and the evil of having too much, of bossing and of being bossed: where did this evil arise and what was the remedy? He knew that socialism could answer neither question correctly, but was convinced that somewhere, somehow, religion could. But he had cut himself off from the religion of his childhood, and had no reason to suppose that Christianity could be the cure for the world's sickness.

> "The churches seemed to be concerned solely with their sectarian games—they hardly seemed to be interested even in feeding the hungry. And if you could not count on the parsons to help to redress even common cruelties and injustices, how much less could you count on them in deeper matters? For that was how it struck me, and that was why eventually I had to leave the Fabian Society also, for I could not believe that charity was the flowering of justice, but, on the contrary it seemed to me, all inarticulate though I was and quite utterly unable to express the matter, that justice was the flowering of charity." Hunt's Abu ben Adhem was all wrong. "You couldn't profess to love your fellow men and know no more. It was damned impudence to start with—damned pharisaism too. I give tithes of all I possess; I give alms—see, boys, in short, how I love my fellow men. That was not at all what was meant when it was said: How can you love God whom you have not seen, if you do not love your neighbour whom you have seen? It means that you must *start* by loving God and, in the light of that love, in that light of love—for God *is* love—and as its necessary and inevitable fruit, you must love your neighbour. But you must love God first. Otherwise your neighbour-love would be a wrong kind of love; it would turn out to be no love at all or simply self-love" (*Auto.*, pp. 151-52).

The churches "seemed to be doing precisely what was forbidden—professing to love God whom they had not seen and yet bearing no fruit in love of neighbours. Their God-love was suspect. Their God himself was suspect. But, on the other hand, my friends, the socialists, were in no better case." They professed love of their neighbour and nescience of God's existence, so how could their love be well founded? Their concrete demands were endless, from higher wages to higher studies, from baths to abolition of privilege; and this conception of a "soup-kitchen world" was opposed, not because it was godless, but because it would cut down profits.

"You can't just demand justice for the poor and leave it at that. You must find out who are the poor and what is 'who', and what is justice that the poor should be given it." It's no good agitating for municipal housing till you have made up your mind what sort of a being it is that has got to be housed. "Is it conceivable that he is a temple of the Holy Ghost? But what the devil is that? And what kind of housing can possibly be his suitable shrine?" (*Auto.*, p. 154). Religion is the first thing necessary; without it there is no answer to the primary and fundamental questions, What is man, and why? But Gill had no religion, and all the ready-made ones were wrangling among themselves, so that even of the Christian churches no two seemed to answer the questions alike. There was therefore nothing for it but for him to make up a religion for himself, or rather a metaphysic, a preamble to religion (considering it schematically).[1] And then he began to discover, very slowly and gradually, that his new invention was an old one. "To invent" means to come upon, to find, to uncover; and what Gill was inventing was, to his surprise and indeed alarm, stripped of all real or assumed irrelevancies, Roman Catholicism.

[1] For more particulars of these conclusions the *Autobiography* gives a reference to *The Highway*, organ of the Workers' Educational Association, November 1910 to February 1911.

> "I did not think so to start with. In fact I thought I was doing quite the opposite. I thought the Christianity of the churches was dead and finished, and surely one can be forgiven for thinking so. The effect of Christianity in the world seemed non-existent, and I knew of Roman Catholicism only by repute. I did not know any Roman Catholics and I hardly ever went into any Roman Catholic churches or even read Roman Catholic books; moreover what little I knew of Roman Catholicism from outward appearances was, in a general way, revolting. . . . I suppose nothing on earth is more completely and efficiently camouflaged than Peter's 'barque', which, from a short distance, looks exactly like the Ritz Palace Hotel." But "I found a thing in my mind and I opened my eyes and found it in front of me. You don't become a Catholic by joining the Church; you join the Church because you are a Catholic" (*Auto.*, 166, 93, 170).

And so in 1913, on his thirty-first birthday, Eric Gill and his wife and three children were received into the Roman Catholic Church.

I am not writing an *apologia pro vita sua* in the sense of that phrase canonized by John Henry Newman (or, for that matter, in any sense). But Gill's becoming a Catholic (or as I, writing as a Roman Catholic, would prefer to put it, his coming into visible fellowship with the Church) was certainly the most important, the most formative, the most integrating and creative factor in his life:[1] and I say this not as a pious *cliché* or expression of sectarian partiality, but as a plain fact which must be patent to anyone who knew him or who studies his work. Moreover his action in this regard has at times been misunderstood or even, in perfect good faith, misrepresented. A little more must therefore be said

[1] Gill ends his autobiography with it: the remaining ninety-one pages, one third of the whole book, are labelled "postscript".

about it, and first, that Gill was never, at any time of his life, an ecclesiastically-minded layman, in the depreciatory sense of that expression; I would even dare to say, at the risk of being misunderstood, that he was not "interested in religion"—but he was passionately in love with God.

"I was never interested in all the stuff my high-church brothers and their friends went in for—synods and councils and the thirty-nine articles of religion, and ritual and vestments and the episcopal succession. That all seemed twaddle to me, and I wasn't interested in the anti-catholic stuff either—Pope Joan and Maria Monk and the Spanish Inquisition, medieval corruption, cardinals' mistresses, superstition and pious frauds. I knew, surely everyone knows, that a man can be a holy man, a good man and an intelligent man, and yet be covered with sores, have a shocking temper and be subject to all the temptations of the flesh" (*Auto.*, p. 170). Religion means the rule of God, and Gill had a vision of a holy church ruling the world in the name of God—not a theocracy in a political but in a personal sense; speaking as one having authority—not authoritarian in principle (whatever the appearance and practice to the contrary), not answering every difficult or tom-fool question, but saying quietly and firmly "*This* is the way of the Lord", and putting the responsibility on her children to walk in it. So it was not professional apologetics or intellectual wrestling or that mythical[1] "aesthetic appeal" or that desire to "escape into an imposed certainty" (of which so much is heard) that persuaded Gill he had

[1] As will be seen in a subsequent paragraph, this epithet does not call in question the beauty of Roman Catholic services, which with the liturgies of worship of other ancient churches form a supreme work of art. But in the average Roman Catholic church they come in for some rough handling, and are disguised by a layer of commercial fripperies, "devotional" externals, and a lack of really corporate approach that faithfully reflect the contemporary world.

found the Church of God: like many another, he found as many problems to cope with after he became a Catholic as before, only they were different problems; as for books, "if any mere book did do anything to make me a Catholic, it is *Bishop Blougram's Apology*", which had been put before him as an anti-Catholic tract. How then did he become convinced? His own account tells us little and that little is not very clear—as is to be expected, for faith and the coming of faith are little more "patient of dialectical exposition" than is God himself. "I would not have anyone think that I became a Catholic because I was *convinced* of the truth, though I *was* convinced of the truth. I became a Catholic because I fell *in love* with the truth, and love is an experience. I saw. I heard. I felt. I tasted. I touched. And that is what lovers do" (*Auto*., p. 247). Certainly he was deeply impressed by the fruits that Christianity had borne amid the corruptions of the dark and middle ages—and there was the Gospel.

> "I had been brought up on the Gospel, so of course I can't say what effect that book would have had on me if it had been possible to approach it entirely from outside. It might be more impressive or it might be less. It is impossible to tell. But the mere fact that you've been brought up with a thing doesn't necessarily give it an unfair pull over your mind. I don't see why it should. It might work just the other way. All I know is that I felt like the prodigal son. I had been away, squandering my substance in riotous living—not with women and wine, though that would have been nice, but with riotous young minds and the wine of strong words—and now I was, in a manner of speaking, coming home. . . . 'The Church proceeds confidently in her doctrine of God'—and not only that, but her doctrine of God inspires confidence. Perhaps the reader doesn't think so. To me it was obvious. The Christ of the Gospel was the Christ of

the Church in spite of all the funny stuff—Vatican paraphernalia, 'repository art', and heathen superstition masquerading as Christian revelation. I boasted to myself that I could see the wood quite plainly in spite of the trees" (*Auto.*, pp. 182-3).

But on pages 186-7 of the *Autobiography*, in the course of an account of a visit to the Benedictine monastery of Mont César at Louvain, there is what seems to this writer a most significant passage. Eric attended one of the conventual offices in the church.

> "At the first impact I was so moved by the chant, which you must remember I had never heard a note of in my life before, as to be almost frightened. . . . This was something alive, living, coming from the hearts and minds and bodies of living men. It was as though God were continuing the work of creation here and now, and I was there to hear, to see—even almost to touch. . . . There, at Louvain, after the slow procession of incoming monks and the following short silence when I first, all unprepared and innocent, heard 'Deus in adiutorium . . .' I knew, infallibly, that God existed and was a living God—just as I knew him in the answering smile of a child or in the living words of Christ."

Many would set this down simply as emotionalism, therefore unreliable and of uncertain value, if not valueless: especially might this be said by those who do not know the timeless, "unearthly" quality of the chant of the Roman church—had it been the "Gloria" of the B-minor Mass or the "Credo" of Gretchaninov the objection would be weightier. And Gill seems to have anticipated the objection, for he goes on: "There is a palpable righteousness in the things that God has made and that man is God's instrument for making. Emotion follows—of course, inevitably, naturally, but emotion is that which is suffered. It is the suffering that follows knowledge. We may, and often do, forget the knowing and wallow only in the emotion. It is better to forget the emotion. And when I got home from Louvain I did forget it and I remembered only that Christianity was 'pas symbolique'."

I know the man; I know the music; I know the occasion: I do not believe that that was emotionalism. The Spirit bloweth where and how he listeth; God is not bound by his own sacraments, he can make a sacrament, an outward vehicle of inward grace, of any created thing: and surely Eric Gill received a sacrament, a "charismatic sacrament", if such an expression be allowable, bearing the grace of light and faith, there in the abbey church of Mont César; the bodiless finger of God, clothed in the materiality of public corporate worship, touched him.

It has been said that all the "denominational" disagreements of Christians flow from one fundamental disagreement about the nature of the Church. It seems that they can indeed be reduced to that and it is therefore worth looking at how the Church appeared to Eric Gill, a man whose convictions attracted people of widely differing views.

> "It has been said that the Church exists in order that words may have a meaning. That, in its ultimate essence, is what a church is, that by which how, when and why cease to be pragmatical catcalls and become intelligible symbols, symbols patient of interpretation" (*Belief*, p. 310). The Church is "a perfectly human institution, matter and spirit, and the primacy is of the spirit, therefore guided by the Holy Ghost, therefore the bride of Christ, therefore a divine institution also. . . . Just as, in my mind, the Christianity

enunciated by St John and St Paul is the necessary complement of the Christianity enunciated by the other evangelists, so the Church as sacrificing priest is the necessary complement of the Church as the living voice. And just as Calvary was the necessary consummation of Christ's life, so the Eucharist is the necessary consummation of our life in him. . . . Our earthly life is symbolized by the bread and wine. Under the appearance of bread and wine God gives himself to us. Thus are we made sharers of his divinity who saw fit to share our humanity. Thus man, who was made in the beginning with the dignity of God's image, is yet more wonderfully renewed" (*Auto.*, pp. 190, 246).

Gill was the last man to confound things that should not be mixed up, to confuse the Church of God with the life and opinions of people, clerical or lay, who profess her membership. None saw more clearly than he the sectarianism (historically explainable) of many Roman Catholics in England, their obsession with such secondary issues as the "schools question", the efforts of their politics to convince an unnecessarily unbelieving generation that Catholics were as keen on the British Empire, mass-production, money-making and wireless culture as anybody else; their shocking complacency: "We alone were good and intelligent, and everyone else was in outer darkness: Protestants, heretics, and either fools or knaves. It was assumed that the Church was hated and Catholics absolutely basked in that hatred, wallowed in it."[1] But he saw no less clearly that the Roman church in England is "a living member of the Universal Church and knows a greatness and a wisdom and a holiness which is entirely unknown to the majority of English people" (*Auto.*, 209, 198).

[1] It must in fairness be recognized, as Gill recognized, that these things have been considerably modified in the past twenty years.

The Church for Gill, then, was the church of the oldest Christian tradition—something which teaches the necessary truths about man's first beginning and last end, wherein fallen and divided man is united, restored and divinized, particularly in the sacramental meal which commemorates and continues the redeeming sacrifice of her Master and Lord.[1] No simply human assembly can do these things; she is divine. Her members on earth, members not in the sense of members of a club, but as a hand of the body or a branch of the tree, visibly or hiddenly united with her, are human: she is human.

Of what can be said against the Roman Catholic Church on her human side he was only too well aware—but "the world" was painfully apparent, even to the length of apostasy and betrayal, among the first Twelve themselves, yet who now would choose the alternative of following Herod and Pilate?

> "When you think of St Peter's and the toy soldiery, and the purple and lace of its fat worldly-looking prelates, and when you think of the subtle intangibilities and intransigencies of its diplomacy, it is not difficult to understand why people run away in a panic—what's it all got to do with the Man on the Ass, anyway? But to me the alternative was too clear to be missed or to be run away from. In fact both alternatives were too clear. The frightful, the truly frightful, horror of the corruption of the ancient Church was as nothing to the essential dirtiness, dirtiness in its very being and nature, of the industrial-capitalist world" (*Auto.*, p. 189).

So he answered the question, the "all-inclusive and final question", "Do you believe all that the holy Church

[1] To discourage individualistic devotion and to emphasize the corporate nature of this act, Gill advocated the putting of the altar in the middle of the church with the congregation all around. See "Mass for the Masses" in *Sacred and Secular*.

teaches?" with an unhesitating "Yes". "But as to *what* she teaches on all the multiplication of funny subjects that we worry ourselves about, well, at the great risk, or rather, certainty of being thought both lazy and unscrupulous, I made up my mind to confine my attention to things that seemed fundamentally important and things that intimately concerned me" (*Auto.*, p. 191). Not for him to trouble his head about whether Jonah really lived inside a fish or whether Pope Honorius I taught heresy or whether Anglican orders are valid—or what "valid" means in that connection.

He had a strong glowing faith, but it was not the faith of a child or of the proverbial Breton peasant—because he was not a child or a Breton peasant. His was the faith of a man of more than common fineness of spirit and intellectual ability, and he had put away childish things. But his understanding of what are and what are not childish things differed greatly from that of the more complacent or unimaginative who quote St Paul on that head—with the result that he was childlike in the sense of Christ's admonition. Playfulness was a trait in his character, "play" was one of his sacred words, and he loved to think of children—and grown-ups—playing before their Father in the streets of the Heavenly Jerusalem. But he would tolerate no prettifying of or toying with the majestic mysteries of the Christian faith and life: in his *Sacred and Secular* can be read a manly and adult application of the "little way" of St Teresa of Lisieux, and a book about the same simple young nun provoked him to a blistering review that was probably as near vituperation as he ever got.

§

For the next four years Gill was principally engaged in carving the fourteen panels called stations of the cross for Westminster Cathedral, the work which put him definitely in the front rank of contemporary English sculptors. Then—it was September 1918—he was conscripted for the army. He was, of course, by now under no illusions about politics, but he had paid no particular attention to the causes and conduct of war or to the congruity or otherwise of Christians engaging in organized violence at the behest of the civil power: his attitude was that warfare and fighting was not his line of business, that if he were really wanted he would be fetched, and then he would go quietly. So he was drafted into the mechanical-transport section of the R.A.F. His military service lasted under four months, but it was a "monstrous and momentous experience". After four years of war the "people's army", especially on home-stations, had been thoroughly militarized and dehumanized, the recruits were unwilling and fed-up from the start (at one camp at which he was stationed there were several suicides a week), and Gill found himself, not with young rustics or tradesmen (in the proper sense of that word) or others with whom he had common interests, but with men from the suburbs of industrial towns, under the worst sort of n.c.o. "If I had not had that brief taste of army life I should never have known what it is like to be one of the 'submerged tenth', an under-dog, a person of no use to anyone but as an instrument, a unit on a pay-sheet . . ." (*Auto.*, p. 205).

After his release Gill returned to work at Ditchling Common, where with friends and their families living in neighbouring houses there was in process of formation a society of Roman Catholics, a gild, bound by their common faith and common ideas about work and society: printing, stone-carving and carpentry were among their trades. The six years that followed are passed over in a very few pages of the *Autobiography*, but they were important in that they saw the beginning and development of Eric's association with the Order of Preachers. The members of the Ditchling gild, though living in independent households, soon found the need of some limited rule of life to be followed by all, and one or other of the third-orders, founded by the friars in the middle ages, was obviously indicated: their choice fell on that one which forms part of the Order of Preachers, "Black Friars", founded by St Dominic in 1215.[1] The principal work of this order is sufficiently indicated by its name: the Dominicans are essentially teachers, and in particular they are exponents of the philosophical and theological teaching and method of St Thomas Aquinas, himself a Dominican, the fine flower of the colossal Christian and intellectual rebirth of the thirteenth century.

Eric became an enthusiastic disciple of Aquinas. This must not be misunderstood. He was never an accomplished thomist, he was not even deeply read in St Thomas's works; he learned his teaching principally in the old way, by word of mouth, from the several Dominican friars who were his lifelong friends and admirers. "The starting-point of human progress," says Christopher Dawson, "is to be found in the highest type of knowledge —the intuition of pure being . . . man's development is not so much from the lower to the higher as from the confused to the distinct." The first need of our time, says Jacques Maritain, is an intellectual need, the need for clarity of understanding. "Good will is not so obviously wanting as good sense," glossed Gill, and agreed with

[1] A third-order, whose members are called "tertiaries", is an association of lay people, not normally living in community, who follow a private rule of life under the direction of an order of mendicant friars. To-day they hardly differ in practice from any other similar religious society; in the middle ages their obligations and significance were more serious.

Dawson and Maritain with passionate intensity. St Thomas as the philosopher of being, as pre-eminently the philosopher of common sense, as a mind of almost unearthly clarity, with a method to match it—that was what first attracted him; and then he found in St Thomas, stated and argued clearly and succinctly as nowhere else, the principles of God and man which Eric used with such devastating force (but not, alas! with corresponding effect) against the politico-industrial set-up of contemporary society. That, I think, both in life and teaching, was the principal preoccupation of the Ditchling days, to show Catholics in particular that the material basis of what is called twentieth-century civilization is fundamentally incompatible not simply with Christianity but with man's natural good: the groundwork was laid of that social teaching which for the rest of his life he put tirelessly, not only before his co-religionists, but before all who were willing to listen. And while Aquinas helped him with metaphysical and psychological principles, he found masterly statements of principles of practice and analyses of the evils of the day in the social pronouncements of two popes, Leo XIII and Pius XI, notably the encyclical-letters "Rerum novarum" and "Quadragesimo anno": documents which, translated into turgid italianate English, explained and explained away time and again, used as slogans and stamping-ground for study clubs instead of springs of action, have lacked the influence they ought to have had in this country.

When his vigorous and mathematically-inclined mind first came under the influence of the presentation of Christianity which owes so much to Western medieval rationalism and Counter-reformation juridicism, when he was first entranced by St Thomas's use of aristotelian logic and categories of thought, Gill ran some danger of becoming too exclusively engrossed in man's rational powers,[1] of believing that all truth can be expressed in syllogistic terms, even of ultimately bogging-down in the morass of legalism:[2] he was in violent revolt from the confused thinking and aesthetic emotionalism of the "art world", from the relativist opportunism of socialist politics, from excessive dependence on religious experience that was not necessarily religious. And he was now coming into contact with people many of whom, with sneers at the alleged muddle-headedness, illogicality and compromise of their fellow Englishmen, continually lauded the alleged realism and logical consistency of Frenchmen and Italians and Roman Catholics in general. But Gill was too fearless, too wide-spirited, too mentally alert to succumb to the danger; if he had too much good sense to confuse prejudice or arbitrary judgement, wishful thinking or emotion, with intuition, so was he too whole a character to underrate the intuitive, the charismatic, the prophetic. This became more pronounced as he got older, and in the year before he died he wrote:

> "The best and the most perfect way is the way of love. This applies not only to life but also to teaching. The best and most perfect way to inculcate, for example, the virtue of honesty is to shew that love implies it. It is probable that no other method can ever be successful; for though we are rational beings, inasmuch

[1] But, as Gill often pointed out, the use of reason is not to be identified with the process of ratiocination. And "the senses are a kind of reason" (he did not invent that saying, he found it in St Thomas).

[2] Early in our friendship he surprised me by saying of the Church's condemnation of a certain action as sinful in essence that "I can't understand *why*. I'm always rebelling against it. Now if it were merely a disciplinary rule, imposed for reasons of expediency, I'd be quite happy about it". Years later he told me that his attitude had become quite the opposite: he had learned to be critical of the desirability and efficacy of rules and regulations and the ingenuities of casuists and canon lawyers. "The more canon law, the less religion" (it was not Gill but an ecclesiastic who said that).

as we are persons . . . yet we use our reason so rarely and fitfully and with so rash a carelessness, without training or discipline; we follow our prejudices and predilections with such confidence and impudence that any appeal based upon rational argument is unlikely to be successful. Moreover the lovely has a wider reference than the reasonable: what we love we do not merely desire—it is something that, whether consciously or not, we recognize to be right as well as good, not only desirable but also as it ought to be; and the fact that this recognition is arrived at by that leap of the intelligence that we call intuition, and not by discursive reasoning and the painful process of thinking it out step by step by logical argument, seems to show that reasoning is both unnecessary and absurd . . ." *Seems to be*, not *is; and*, not *or*.

And, as Walter Shewring has emphasized (*Blackfriars*, February 1941, pp. 87–89), Eric increasingly disassociated himself from that strong obscurantist party that refuses to look outside the Roman Catholic Church for any assistance whatever in the pursuit of truth. "He accepted every consequence of the Ambrosian principle embraced by St Thomas, that *all* truth is from the Holy Ghost." No one was to think that "when I affirm the truth of Christianity I am therefore denying the truth of other faiths—at the most I am only denying their denials" (*Machine Age*, p. 19). There was no question of minimizing Christian doctrine: "Of all truths, the truth dearest to Eric Gill was that of the Incarnation. . . . But he responded eagerly to the call of such exponents of Eastern wisdom as Ananda Coomaraswamy (a venerated friend) and René Guénon"; and the present writer can testify to his eagerness to learn from the Eastern Christian tradition and mentality, with which, indeed, he came to have some close affinities.

Gill and his family left Ditchling Common in 1924[1] or a more remote and undisturbed home in a valley of he Black Mountains in Breconshire. Two other families ccompanied them from Ditchling and there was another f friends already there, but no attempt was made at any rganization or communal living beyond what is necesarily involved by common interests and close contiguity. Iere, at Capel-y-ffin, he did little stone-carving but a lot f lettering and wood-engraving and there was the beginaing of his great work as a designer of printing-types, vork which brought him into association with that "busiiess-world" he so often attacked: it is an appreciative eference to the Monotype Corporation in the *Autobioraphy* that brings forth his disclaimer (often repeated lsewhere) of any intention to impute malice and wickedess to any individual man of business, so many of whom e had met were "more than nice", men with inherited raditions of honesty and good service trying to maintain hose traditions within a system that must prove fatal to hem sooner or later. However strongly he spoke of the usiness world or "the rich" or the sufferings of the vorkers, what he really had his eye on was not the iniquiies of individual persons but an organization of society ı which they are all unavoidably tied up, which, whether e knows it or not, bears in its way as hardly on Henry ord as on Bill Jones: there must be justice for dukes (if here be any) as much as for dustmen—and in either case ıstice is due to them precisely as men, human beings. In nother book of this series F. A. Lea writes of G. K. hesterton that, "What he beheld was not the calculated xploitation of one class by another, but an all-pervading ıjustice accepted as a matter of course nearly as much

[1] The Ditchling gild still exists. Its press published the first work in nglish of that great Frenchman Jacques Maritain, viz., *Art et Scolasque*, translated by the Reverend John O'Connor under the title "The ilosophy of Art".

by the 'proletarian' as the capitalist. What he strove to create was a general consciousness of its existence, equal to his own, so that it must either become deliberate and challenging, or else be rectified, by the substitution of co-operation for competition." This is exactly true of Gill (though he would not refer to his "revolution" in such equivocal terms: competition is sometimes good, and there can be co-operation for evil).

§

As he grew older Eric Gill gave more and more attention to the problem of man in society, the question both social and religious of how persons can lead a whole, and therefore at least potentially holy, life on this earth. He was always a most strenuous and fully-occupied worker, but latterly screwed out ever more time for books, articles and lectures directly or indirectly concerned with this theme. With, I believe, very little conscious missionary purpose, this son of missionaries and brother of the Friars Preachers expounded Christian principles and practice in places where they would otherwise hardly, or never, have been heard.[1] He accepted invitations to speak or write, on this or that aspect of work and art or on social problems or on peace and war, indifferently for Catholics and Quakers, capitalists and communists, official bodies and obscure groups. This high-tide of lecturing came later, but it was at Capel-y-ffin that writing began to have a notable part in his activities, his pamphleteering, as he called it. His earlier publications were single essays; then came collections of articles reprinted from numerous periodical publications, many of them little known; and

[1] "The deep religion of his teaching has been to me literally the revelation of a new gospel," wrote Dr. Mulk Raj Anand in his *Hindu View of Art*.

then longer single essays, *e.g.*, on clothes, on typography, culminating in two full-length books, *The Necessity of Belief*[1] and the *Autobiography*.

These writings give a very clear and, on the whole, adequate account of Gill's ideas and arguments; and they are remarkable not only for their internal consistency but for their consistency and correlation as a whole: from the few paragraphs on Slavery and Freedom written in 1918 down to the posthumously published autobiography he was "telling the same story", often in the same words. He was not afraid of repeating himself: "It has been said that I am one of those writers who can only keep to the point by returning to it. I may say in self-defence that there are many readers who can only remember the point if it is repeated often enough" (*Beauty*, p. 5); in particular, certain pregnant "sayings" and quotations with which every reader of Eric Gill is familiar occur in the earliest writings as in the latest: such, for example, are "Look after goodness and truth, and beauty will look after herself", "Man is made up of body and spirit, both real and both good", St Augustine's "Love, and do what you will". The same basic ideas are always there—the nature of man and his relation to God, the Christian revelation, human responsibility and therefore the necessity of freedom, human sin and divine grace, man's work as a calling to collaborate with God in creation—and it seems to me that in general their application underwent but little real development: what did develop was Eric Gill himself; he saw the same things but saw deeper into them, he saw farther and he saw more clearly, and in that vision he wrote about the same things again.

There can also be found in Gill's writings, especially

[1] He disliked this title as pretentious, and wanted to call it "Believe It or Not". His publishers, Messrs. Faber & Faber, would not agree, but he had his way with the subtitle. *See* bibliography.

the *Autobiography*, about as good a picture of what a man was like as can be got without knowing him in person—except in one particular (and here I except the *Autobiography* and, in a measure, *The Necessity of Belief*): his actual style of writing and expressing himself was not always *l'homme même*, it was often misleading. It is sometimes said by those who did not know him personally that Gill was intolerant, dogmatic (in the vulgar sense) and contemptuous of those who disagreed with him: an obituary-writer who ought to have known better attributed to him a mythical "rich flow of invective". It is easy to see how hasty readers formed this misconception: as he often admitted, in and out of print, his manner of writing could give an impression of cocksureness, of laying down the law. But it was a laughably wrong impression, for not the least remarkable thing about Eric was his humility and a diffidence that was sometimes staggering. While never deferring to an opinion, by whomever expressed, unless and until he came to agree with it, he would ask and listen to the opinion of all and sundry on whatever topic turned up, even on technical matters of his own work. I have seen him bring a handful of engraving proofs in to the evening meal and ask for the criticism of all present —the family, visitors, servants: and next morning some of the suggestions of those inexpert critics were carried out. This humbleness of mind is well illustrated by the following passage from a letter written a few weeks before his death.

> "I've been in bed off and on since April 15 and never anything very serious . . . Old age coming on I guess. Anyway it gave me time and opportunity to write book for Cape as ordered—100,000 words about my so-called 'life'. He asked for an autobiography but I told him it couldn't be done: it would have to be an 'autopsychography', and that's what it is. . . . Really it amounts to

a 'search for the City of God', but of course I can't give it a fine title like that. . . . It feels to me as though I ought really to die now. I don't know how I shall be able to face the world after stripping myself more or less naked as I have done."

Since the publication of that 'autopsychography' there is no longer any excuse for thinking Eric Gill bumptious and intolerant.

Gill had hammered out in his mind and tested by practice certain principles, and these he put forward tirelessly for consideration and debate. But he hated to appear to be taking upon himself what he regarded as an office primarily of the clergy, and for that reason, as well as for the sake of first principles and of those who do not accept Christianity, he would appeal to natural reason as often as, or more often than, to divine revelation, to justice rather than to charity: charity he lived, his passion for justice was a fruit of his intense lovingness, and in more intimate private talk he would speak of God and of love more often than of either justice or reason. His intellectual judgements were downright ("We are told not to cast pearls before swine," he said, "And to adjudge persons swine in this sense necessitates making an intellectual judgement of them"), but he was always scrupulous to try to avoid making, or seeming to make, moral judgements of persons. I do not recollect ever hearing him utter a word intended to wound, and time and again I have watched him trying to find a worthy explanation of someone's apparently indefensible action, or gently changing the conversation when another's character or deeds were coming in for rough handling. Some years ago he and I were invited to speak in support of the war-resisters' candidate for the lord-rectorship of Glasgow University. The audience was extremely disorderly and Gill (who had a poor delivery) was hardly heard: I, by hardening my heart and being rude, forced some sort of hearing. "The difference between the two speakers," commented a Presbyterian minister afterwards, "was that Gill was forgiving those hooligans all the time, whereas Attwater did not forgive them till he had finished." Very characteristic of Gill; so, too, was his bewilderment that intelligent young people (he was extremely sympathetic towards the young, but without a trace of the "Youth" ramp) could come to a serious meeting only in order to make a din.

The last twelve years of his life Gill lived in Buckinghamshire, twelve full and fruitful years in which, by unflagging work and perfect order in the conduct of his affairs, his thought, writing and lecturing were enabled to keep pace with his stone carving and typography.[1] One of the carving jobs was ten panels for the new museum at Jerusalem, which involved two longish visits to Palestine, which must be spoken of here because his stay there was the last of several things in his life that he regarded as "revelations".

Many people go to Palestine and come back having apparently seen nothing but flies and touts, dirt and "backwardness", the rivalries of religions and the quarrels, emulations and meannesses of their sects. All these things are there and in good measure, and Eric saw them, but

[1] Among his stone works (not all at this time) were stations of the cross in churches at Bradford and Leatherhead, the Leeds University war memorial, and carvings for the underground station at St. James's Park, at Broadcasting House, and for the League of Nations building at Geneva. He was also commissioned for work on the new Anglican cathedral at Guildford. He designed eleven faces of printing type, including a Greek, a Hebrew and an Arabic face. He engraved (on wood) many decorations for the books of the Golden Cockerel, Count Kessler's, and other presses. He was made an associate of the Royal Academy, an honorary member of the Royal Institute of British Architects, an LL.D., *honoris causa* of Edinburgh University, and was one of the original recipients of the new designer-for-industry honour (!). Some even of his friends did not know of these recognitions, which he regarded simply as manifestations of the uncritical kindness of the public bodies concerned.

there are other things to be seen, and he saw them too. "In the Holy Land I saw a holy land indeed; I also saw, as it were eye to eye, the sweating face of Christ. . . . To me it was like living with the Apostles. It was like living in the Bible." And the beauty he saw was of people, of the Palestinian "Arabs" living without pride and with dignity in their poverty, sinful but humanly sinful; of places, Galilee and the Jordan wilderness; of the work of men's hands, above all of that Moslem shrine, the Haram as-Sharif at Jerusalem, which he declared to be the most beautiful place he had ever seen, the most spiritually pervaded. "Tell me where there is another. Is it in London, in Trafalgar Square? Is it the Place de la Concorde? Is it on the Acropolis at Athens? They tell me that is very lovely, but at Jerusalem living men worship the living God; at Athens there is but a memory of what was. Is it even in the piazza of St Peter's? No, not there. . . ."

As for the shrines of Christendom, the basilica of Bethlehem, reminder also of the pride and glory of blood-stained Byzantium, the church of the Holy Sepulchre, reminder also of the brutalities and arrogance of Western Europe breaking in on Asia—these he would rather have as they were, half-ruinous, cluttered with the ecclesiastical junk of half a dozen churches, dirty and profaned, than restored and polished up by Caesar's building-contractors. "By the inscrutable decree of God the sweat is not thus to be wiped from His face"; the squabblings of Catholics and Orthodox, Armenians and Greeks, do less dishonour to Christ than if they should abandon his cross entirely and "hand the whole notion of salvation to the sanitary authority", as our civilization seeks to do. Jerusalem has "not yet rendered to Caesar the things that are God's" (*Auto.*, pp. 281, 257).

Blessed are the poor, for theirs is the Kingdom of God:

that truth was first taught in the Holy Land and Gill found that it can still be learned there to-day, and he came back with his mind made up. "Henceforward I must take up a position even more antagonistic to my contemporaries than that of a mere critic of the mechanistic system. I must take a position antagonistic to the very basis of their civilization. And I must appear antagonistic even to the Church itself. Of course that is all nonsense but that is how it must appear. For the Christians everywhere have committed themselves to the support of capitalist industrialism and therefore to the wars in its defence, mechanized war to preserve mechanized living, while I believe that capitalism is robbery, industrialism is blasphemy and war is murder " (*Auto*., p. 257). It was with these convictions, more or less clearly envisaged, that Eric Gill had lived most of his life; and with them thus reinforced, seen as it were from a Pisgah height between the hill of redemptive Death and the tomb of bodily and spiritual Resurrection—the spot in which Palestinian folk-wisdom so aptly recognized the centre of the world—he worked out his few remaining earthly years.

He died in a hospital close to London, in the night of November 17–18, 1940. An air raid was going on.

2

CHRISTIAN revolutionary. It was characteristic of Eric Gill that when something came up for discussion he would seek at once a definition of terms, and that as a starting-point for such definition he would consult the dictionary for the etymology and current meanings of the words concerned—the "Concise Oxford" was always kept handy. Turning, then, to the "Shorter Oxford", I find under *Christian*, "one who follows the precepts and example of Christ"; this, with the addition of "tries to" before "follow", is very suitable for my purpose. Under *revolutionary* I find "[one who works for or advocates] the complete overthrow of the established government in any country or state by those who were previously subject to it: a forcible substitution of a new ruler or form of government".

That Gill was a sincere and fervent *Christian* in the above wide sense needs no demonstration, nor that he was one in a more strict sense; for he voluntarily united himself with the Roman Catholic Church: and, whatever may be thought of some passages in her history, of some of her teaching and still more of the teaching of some of her theologians, of some of her practice and still more of the practice of many of her members, that church as a whole must be recognized as an unflinching upholder throughout the centuries of the traditional fundamental truths of Christian faith and life. Gill, therefore, professed no eclectic or dilettante Christianity: he sought to follow Christ, not, for example, as the world's most attractive or convincing ethical teacher, but because he believed him to be the One God, clothed in human flesh, with all that follows from that stupendous concept.

Two possible misunderstandings may here be cleared up. On the one hand, he was no doctrinaire religionist, no sectarian peddler of the beliefs of his church as a sort of spiritual and religious patent-medicine which would cure all ills by the simple swallowing; he never flourished the Catholic faith like a tomahawk. He believed that faith with all his heart and soul, and he never forgot it is part of that faith that its dogmas must be lived as well as assented to before they can bear fruit. "To be religious means to believe in order, and order implies a person ordering"—God: and "a great religious period is one in which men proceed confidently in a doctrine of God". He believed ("We do not claim that what we believe is true because we believe it, but simply that what we believe is what we hold to be certain"), he believed that God ordained a teaching church on earth—but that does not involve belief in every word that proceeds from the mouth of her theologians (who in any case not seldom contradict one another): "theologians have not infrequently made confusion where their job was to clear things up. They have collected the butterly only to kill it and pin it down, and the meaning they have pinned down has turned out to be not the real meaning but only that one which was suitable for such pinning."

On the other hand, neither was Gill "anti-clerical". In the continental sense of the expression, which involves opposition to a given church or even to Christianity itself, obviously he was not: in the English sense, which seems ultimately to convey the idea that clergymen necessarily know less about true religion than anybody else, his words sometimes appear to be strongly imbued with it. I do not refer to such good-humoured digs as that "[the problem of evil is such that] even theologians have been humble before it", but to harder sayings: for instance, that the swagger, human prowess and greatness implied by the church architecture of Renaissance Rome is more defiling to the face of Christ than our contemptuous spittle. "The nonsensical and illusory grandeurs of Rome, Rome, the Holy City, decked out in the finery of ballrooms and banks, the soul-ensnaring magnificence of statistical display, the grand appearance of doctrinal and ethical unity . . . it seemed to me that we should do better to eschew our grandeurs and forget our numbers—and brag less about unity while, to the heathen and the pagans and the infidels, the most conspicuous thing about Christians is their sectarian disunity. . . . For while we fight among ourselves about doctrine, we are united in the common worship of money and material success. Here I do not exaggerate. That is the awful thing" (*Auto.*, p. 254). "The clergy are in the position of men standing on the brink of a frozen pool and shouting to men drowning under the ice that they should take good deep breaths if they want to be healthy" (*M. & M.*, p. 36). "The clergy are everywhere acknowledged to be custodians of faith and morals—the faith is what you more or less blindly believe because your school-teachers taught it during 'religious instruction', and morals are little more than a list of things you mustn't do. Man as an intelligent and intellectual being is hardly mentioned, and never expected to function" (*W. & P.*, p. 100). "It must be a commonplace of our experience that the widespread scepticism of our time is as much the consequence of loss of respect for the preachers of Christ as it is of the writings and teachings of unbelievers, and that that loss of respect is a necessary preliminary" (*Auto.*, p. 104). Many clergy (and others) don't like people to say that sort of thing: the fact that it is true makes it worse.

For the teaching office of the Church, for the priestly office of its ministers, Gill had the profoundest reverence and respect, because it is a special participation in the one true universal priesthood of Jesus Christ (and he was very alive to the truth that every Christian in his measure shares in that priesthood). But this is not to say that the mistakes, exaggerations, deficiencies of persons exercising authority in holy orders should be extenuated or ignored, that as a matter of discipline it is good to treat clergy as outside criticism: that is obscurantism, weakness, laziness, and produces that "clericalism" of which a French archbishop has recently declared, "the Church disapproves of it and we don't want any of it at any price". Moreover, accusations against churches and ecclesiastical authorities can be substantiated only by Christian doctrine. "If you are amazed by the policeman-like frame of mind of many of the clergy and their apparent conviction that the spirit killeth but the letter quickeneth (so that you would think getting to Heaven was a business of going by the book !) you must still remember that the opposite doctrine is Christian teaching, and that it is the authority to which they themselves appeal who is the judge" (*Auto.*, p. 255).

The above-quoted definition of *revolutionary* would certainly never fit so gentle and unpolitically-minded a person as Gill, but in our day the scope of the word has been much extended, to include those who seriously oppose any widely-accepted and well-established state of affairs or social or other system and the principles and philosophy pertinent to it. I suspect that the word started life as a term of abuse, which would account for its definition in negative terms: now that it has become domesticated it is better defined positively, as, say, "an advocate of principles and policies which involve the overthrow or reversal of established systems, etc." And in this wider sense Gill was unquestionably a revolutionary. Not that he used the word much or thought of himself in such terms: in *Work and Property* is an essay called "Art and Revolution" which would be extremely puzzling to most revolutionaries: only at the end does he refer to them at all—and then to dismiss them as mere "progressives"! His reference to his own "little revolution" has already been quoted (p. 15); nevertheless to bring that about would mean "the complete destruction of a civilization in which money is god and men of commerce are our rulers". But "this destruction will come about without any need for 'revolutionary' activity. Let no one suppose I propose to wave a red flag. The present civilization is founded upon an unnatural condition and will come to a natural end. If there are battles, murders and sudden deaths it will not be the fault of"[1]—men like Eric Gill. "A kingdom not of this world"; "Poverty, chastity and obedience"—such were the slogans on the banners of *his* revolt. "These may sound strange watchwords for revolutionists. Consider then the alternatives: Riches, pleasure and irresponsibility, and a kingdom not founded in Heaven!" (*Art Nonsense*, p. 108).

The word "revolution" as commonly used connotes physical violence, and both those who fear and those who welcome the thing like to think of it in terms of the barricades. But the dictionary gives also a more fundamental meaning, "The action of turning over in the mind; consideration; reflection". And it is here that Gill really belongs: "the spirit has the primacy". What he fought for was a "unanimous society", one in which there is unity of *mind* among the people, "who know the same truth and will the same good": what he fought against was the evil *frame of mind* in contemporary society, one that is radically unchristian and antichristian, therefore contrary to nature and to nature's God, "as anti-God as any atheist could wish".

[1] He wrote this in 1928 (*Art Nonsense*, p. 291); I quote it in 1941.

Yes, a Christian revolutionary. And not a revolutionary who happened to be a Christian, or in spite of being a Christian, but revolutionary *because* Christian.

§

Gill being so many-sided a person (each side marvellously correlated with each other), and we humans having a boundless capacity to misunderstand and misinterpret one another, it may clear the picture somewhat to state and explain some of the things that he was *not*, or that he was not in the usual sense of the terms used. The use of labels, especially of ill-defined labels, to tag on to people, whether to express a judgement, favourable or unfavourable, or to pigeonhole them away in what are assumed to be meaningful categories, is one of the minor pernicious diseases endemic in our time.

"The individual rebel, however unspotted from the world he may keep himself, is bound to be tainted by idiosyncrasy and eccentricity; he is likely to be both a prig and a faddist. He will set up for himself a standard of his own making, unless he first ally himself to truth, and truth is a 'who' and not a 'what'!" (*Art Nonsense*, p. 123). Eric did not "ally" but submitted himself to Him who is Truth, and thus was his mind kept purged of idiosyncrasy and eccentricity, priggery and faddism—he was no individualistic crank (certain peculiarities of dress and the like to the contrary notwithstanding). But more of this will be said when I come to speak of his ordinariness and feeling for the "common man", as also then of his freedom from that lop-sided mental superiority that we call "being highbrow" and the fidgety self-conscious "culture" that goes with it.[1] "We are all,"

[1] Gill might well have echoed Göring's famous remark about culture and a revolver. But whereas Göring would shoot down the good men, Gill would shoot down the bogus things. *See* again later.

he said, "so many sweethearts to God. Are we going to fob him off with borrowed kisses—with even the best Elizabethan love-songs? Would he not rather have the vulgar endearments which are our own?" Gill mixed much and sympathetically with cranks and highbrows and *exaltés* of all kinds, and it is not surprising that he has been labelled (sometimes mutually exclusively) with some of their enthusiasms.

He is, for example, commonly regarded as a back-to-the-lander, and it is true that he lived by choice in the country, had the deepest regard for its people and their work, and said, not once but repeatedly, that "The salvation of England cannot be brought about by town improvements; it can only come by the land". But precisely because "the town, the holy city, is nourished upon elements drawn from the soil. The modern towns of our industrial England have no such nourishment".

> "It *is* a lot of nonsense, all this cackle about the beauty of the country. And the cackle would never have been heard if the towns had not become such monsters of indecency and indignity. The town properly thought of is the very crown and summit of man's creativeness. . . . The countryside exists to support and uphold and nourish and maintain the city. . . . Thus the call to the land, to the earth, is the necessary first call. We must be born again, and we must be born again on the land, to dig the earth, to plant and cultivate, to be shepherds and swineherds, to hew wood and draw water, to build simple dwellings and simple places of prayer. But we need not therefore be blinded to what is the truth. Because Babylon is vile it does not follow that Jerusalem is vile also" (*Auto.*, pp. 230–8).

That is not the language of that often rather sentimental state of mind that has earned the contemptuous epithet "back-to-the-landery"; and Gill, while sympathizing with and admiring the heroism of those who follow a call to undertake an agricultural "simple life" in groups and associations, refused the gross over-simplification of regarding this as a cure-all to be urged on people indiscriminately: in particular did he protest against any "attempt to make out that a certain kind of simple, self-supporting country life is the only life for good Christian people" (*Beauty*, p. 34).

Gill had a great appreciation of "that most manly of great men", William Morris (as for Ruskin, who spoke the truth "more eloquently than Cobbett or Disraeli, and more solemnly"), and he was inevitably mixed up in the arts-and-crafts movement. But he had to repudiate it—and was told by the late W. R. Lethaby ("Who shall measure the greatness of this man?") that he was "crabbing his mother". But Gill was not begotten of that movement, and he saw unerringly its two great weaknesses: being unable to compete with mass-production, its products were luxury articles, bought only by the well-to-do; and it positively helped the industrial producers, who copied its designs in their factories and thus started a flood of shams that still further corrupted people's judgement of the times. So Gill escaped from arts-and-crafts: "I'm no gentleman and I don't understand loyalty to lost causes when the causes deserve to be lost."

And he was no medievalist, in the common sense of an uncritical admirer who sees in the middle ages an ideal of life and achievement—Merrie England and all that—which we should in some mysterious way seek to restore or at least approximate to. He associated himself with a religious order medieval in its origin and some of its existing customs—but it is also one of the most up-to-date; he sat at the feet of Aquinas—but Aquinas was a man of universal and timeless mind; he often referred to medieval conditions and practice for illustration, contrast and commendation—but there was nothing specifically medieval about his own dominating ideas. "I do not cite the middle ages because they were good ages or because, in those ages, a certain set of ideas were held to be just and seemly. I do not 'cite' them at all. I am merely describing. . . ." (*Art*, p. 37). Christianity teaches that the enemies of peace and good order are self-seeking and injustice, and for centuries that teaching bore fruit in the subordination of commerce, the outlawry of usury, the upholding of law that defended persons and families as such and evolved the noble concept of the *liber et legalis homo*, "free and lawful man" (now being rapidly superseded, as Richard O'Sullivan, K.C., pertinently remarks, by that of the "insured (or insurable) person"). Gill did not say that that teaching never failed in its effect or that its fruit was always plentiful; but it was after, and with the help of, the Renaissance and the Reformation that commerce and mercantile imperialism became insubordinate and the results of money-lending were honoured, poverty became a disgrace and the rich man as such was esteemed, the workman became on the one hand the artizan and on the other the artist, men gave God's glory to man. Nevertheless, "I am not advocating any indiscriminate praise of pre-Renaissance or pre-industrial works. The seeds of our worship of riches were sown long before Luther or James Watt. A great deal of medieval cathedral-building was no more than human swank and aggrandizement" (*W. & P.*, p. 136), and the religion and law of the middle ages were disfigured by any amount of wickedness, superstition and violent tyranny.

There was a time when Gill could hardly bring himself to use the word "artist", otherwise than as a term of opprobrium; the artist as a special kind of man, the lap-dog of the rich and great, the aesthetician ("relations of masses" and all that), the exploiter of temperament and sensibility, the beauty-wallah—he was certainly not that kind of artist; he was a workman, a carver of stone. The beauty of God is the cause of the being of all that is, said St Thomas, and earthly beauty is no mere delightfulness, or its perception a matter of emotion: it is "that order in things which we perceive to be in itself and at once both right and good. It is perceived by intuition and the knowledge of it is developed by contemplation" (*Art Nonsense*, p. 102); it is the splendour or radiance by which being is manifest, the shiningness perceived in things which are made as they should be; all well-made things are beautiful. "A beautiful thing is that which, being seen, pleases," and there is a whole essay in *Art Nonsense* (pp. 143–158) expounding this apparently simple, if not jejune, definition of Aquinas. "Beauty cannot be taught, and it is best not talked about. It must be spontaneous. It cannot be imposed. . . . Its enemies are irreligion and the offspring of irreligion—commercialism and the rule of the trader" (*Art Nonsense*, p. 94). To recognize it we must use our minds: just as a good life is a mortified life, so "good taste" (as we say) is mortified taste, that is, "taste in which the stupid, the sentimental, the irrelevant is *killed*."

This is not the beauty, this is not the culture, talked about in the "art world" and the welfare departments of philanthropic industrialists and the caverns of the B.B.C. Human culture is the product of necessary work, not of formal education or the activities of leisure hours ("hobbies"): it cannot be plastered on to mankind like an "ornament" glued on to a Woolworth mirror. "To hell with culture, culture as a thing added like a sauce to otherwise unpalatable stale fish! The only culture worth having is that which is the natural and inevitable product of an honourable life of honourable work" (*S. & S.*, p. 173). The divorce of beauty from usefulness and work from culture is an achievement of the bourgeois mind "and there will never be an end of the bourgeois until we have abolished Art", the art of the "art world".

It has been said (*Blackfriars*, February 1941, p. 26) that "one of the difficulties of Eric Gill's position (it was also his strength) was that in his social writings, and increasingly in the later works, his preoccupation was moral, and, if we understand his metaphysics rightly, exclusively moral." That is perfectly true; and yet Gill was emphatically not a moralist in the vulgar sense. He did not go around telling people what they should or should not do, deciding what was right or wrong, sinful or good; he did not identify religion with personal rectitude alone. He knew perfectly well that they cannot be separated, that his own teaching on this, that and the other had immediate and far-reaching implications for personal morality; but his shyness, his humility and his fear lest he trespass on another man's job made him time and again repudiate any intention of talking about morals: his appeal was to good sense rather than to good will, and it was not till comparatively late that he found himself unable to keep silent when silliness, culpable ignorance, falsity or unlovingness had to be identified with sin and that he would refer boldly to the pertinent words of St James or St Paul or our Lord himself.

"'Patriotism is not enough'—morality is not enough. Man is not merely a moral being. He is not merely moral or immoral. He does not merely will good or evil. He also knows true or false: at least he is capable of doing so. And not only does man know and will, he also loves" (*W. & L.*, p. 115). That was a common approach. In one of his attacks on the idea of the "leisure state" he declared: "It is not a moral problem. Leisure is not a problem because people are not good enough to use it properly"; it is an intellectual problem, of what to do that is worth doing. He deprecated the moral fervour that was mixed up with the arts-and-crafts and land movements: morally the handicraftsman or farm-labourer is in precisely the same position as any responsible chemist or engineer. When he deplored the deceits and shams of gothic-revival architecture he was accusing nobody of sin; his appeal was to reason—such things are foolish: "My indignation is not so much a product of moral rectitude as of intellectual exasperation." Nor did he fail to note the weak ineffectiveness of religiose moralism: "Instead of doing anything about economics the moralists fulminate against the murder of unborn children and the selfishness of modern young people [in the practice of birth-prevention]. As somebody said: 'The drains are smelling—let's have a day of intercession'. And as another said: 'The economic depression is a good thing—it is sent to try us'" (*M. & M.*, p. 28). No wonder Pope Pius XI had to mourn that the people at large are estranged from the Church. It is not by moralism or formalist dogmatism, any more than by socialism or the "first-aid" of humanitarianism, that a sick world can be brought to health: "No 'welfare-work' in East London slums will supply religion with a reason of being otherwise lacking. No distribution of property or nationalization of the means of production, distribution and exchange will produce Jerusalem in England's green and pleasant land if the earthly paradise have no City of God for its model. No truth, no good, no beauty will shine out of human handiwork unless the truth that 'whosoever will lose his life shall save it' be known, willed and loved" (*Belief*, p. 304).

Repeatedly from 1936 onwards Eric Gill spoke and

wrote against war, on the platforms and in the publications of the Peace Pledge Union, of Pax and of other associations of war-resisters—yet, though he freely used the term of himself for convenience, he was no pacifist as the word is currently understood. He held that taking part in warfare is not of itself and essentially at variance with a profession of Christianity, that the concept of the possible just war is a valid one, in the conditions commonly received (and usually very imperfectly examined) by Roman Catholics and others: this position Gill held *ex animo*, it appealed to him as traditional, authoritative, reasonable and true. But the more he saw of the contemporary world, the more he learned about political and economic forces, the more that "scientific" means of warfare developed, so much the more he became disturbed in mind. Gradually he began to realize that, as Lord Grey had said, "War is the same word as it was a century ago, but it is no longer the same thing"; the spiritual insight and logic of the medieval and seventeenth-century theologians had been applied to a quite different thing: is it possible to fulfil their conditions for a justifiable war in the new conditions? Gill decided that it is not (and here he parted company from the great majority among those of his co-religionists who have given the matter a moment's thought). He still did not say that no war has ever been justified, that the use of military force is always wrong: he said that war as we know it to-day is such that no human being, much less a Christian, should take part in it; it has become bestial, inhuman, and to talk of patriotism and the defence of civilization by such means is irrelevant. "Modern war is a remedy worse than any conceivable disease"; it is no remedy at all for the congeries of diseases which at present afflict the world: it is an extension and amplification of them. Whatever high-minded, great-souled, public-spirited combatants may intend or do, war is supremely harmful to man's love of God and his fellows, to the spirit of truth and righteousness and justice, to human responsibility and to creative work: depersonalization is at its height and at no other time are men so stirred to undiscriminating hate and abandoned to irrational processes.

"What is the alternative of which we are so afraid? . . . Are we afraid of national humiliation, are we afraid to be humbled? But it is written 'Blessed are the meek, for they shall inherit the earth.' Are we afraid of poverty? But it is precisely poverty which as Christians we should welcome. There will be no peace, there can be no peace, while wealth, comfort, riches are the ideal we set before ourselves" (*Peace*, p. 11). This had been a foremost idea in his mind when he came back from Palestine: "It became clear that it is no use renouncing war unless we first of all renounce riches. That is the awful job before us. . . . A whole world doomed to perpetual fighting—and no remedy but to persuade it to renounce riches. What a forlorn hope!" (*Auto.*, p. 256). Indeed, Gill was more interested in the causes of war than in the strictly moral problem of war itself: all over his later writings are scattered references showing the inevitability of the sort of wars we have in the sort of world we live in—and we all help to make that world.

"Let peacemakers remember above all that it is no manner of good preaching peace unless we preach the things that make for peace—that even the love of our fellow men is no good unless it means giving rather than taking, yielding rather than holding, sharing rather than exclusive possession, confederation rather than sovereignty, use rather than profit. And it means the subordination of the man of business and the dealer and moneylender, both in the world and even more in our own hearts" (in *The Christian Pacifist*, January 1940).

Gill's thought on war, coming later in life, is set out with less system and detail than his other dominant ideas. His insistence on the foulness and shameful vulgarity in all departments of war as waged to-day laid him open to the charge that he was letting his feelings of disgust run away with him, and he was sometimes misunderstood in this way: it is therefore necessary to emphasize that he did not condemn modern war simply because it is horrible. It is a question of means: he denied that spiritual goods can be obtained by killing and hate and destruction, and he vindicated the right of any man to refuse to take part in such an undertaking. "Could not Christ have called on twelve legions of angels to fight for him? And he did not. And shall we think to make a Christian triumph by calling up twelve armies equipped with all the products of our commercialism?—guns, bombs, poisons! (We can only obtain such things by calling in the financiers and borrowing their money.) Shall we thus 'make the world safe for Christianity'?" (*Stations*, p. 5.)

In this context, of the horrors of war, it may be noted in passing that Gill's treatment of the problem of evil is far from satisfactory. He devotes a special chapter to it in *The Necessity of Belief*, and it contains some most valuable analysis and observations, especially the emphasis on the necessity of the distinction between moral and physical evil. There is also a third kind, which may be called spiritual evil, but to treat them, as he seems to do, as being in watertight compartments is bad psychology (and incidentally weakens his own arguments against modern war). The whole thing is badly oversimplified. "There is no problem of evil," he concludes, "There is only the intellectual difficulty of understanding the physical universe and the moral difficulty of withstanding our own appetites and lusts." But surely that precisely is the problem of evil.

§

Having, I hope, cleared up a few possible misunderstandings by this brief reference to some negatives, I turn to a single, and more persuasive and significant, positive: Eric Gill was an "ordinary man", a man-in-the-street, both in his estimate of himself and in fact. "I am," he said, "an ordinary person who refuses to be bamboozled. . . . What concerns me first of all is what man, the common man, the man in the street, the man in the workshop, the man on the farm, claims for himself. After all, I believe it is true to say that the philosopher and the prophet do not claim for man what he does not claim for himself" (*Belief*, p. 227). He assumed no authority to teach: "The most I claim is to speak as one of the people, and as one for whom *vox populi* is *vox Dei*. It is not my voice, it is the people's voice. I claim that what I say is what mankind says. It is no little flock that proclaims man's free will. It is no minority of peculiar persons that asserts man's being" (*Belief*, p. 331). Worms are apt to get the best view of the roots of things, and the important criticism of things as they are to-day comes not from princes and bishops, poets and politicians, but from "man the worm, man the proletarian, man the delectable whore". Early in 1939 the Royal Institution of Great Britain invited four well-known people, of whom Gill was one, to address its members on the relations of art and industry; and he told the assembly that it was a pity that a labourer from a factory had not been asked to speak as well (the address is reprinted in *Sacred and Secular*). On all sides we see men in revolt, and the principal instigators of rebellion in our time have been, not the professed revolutionaries, however important, but those "little men" who "wrote, in cheap books and parish magazines, or preached, in nonconformist chapels, country churches or inconspicuous papist pulpits, the humane doctrine of responsibility for sin and the dual but undivided nature of man."

> They were not conscious agitators, "but they did in fact prevent the entire submergence of the proletariat in the non-human system of industrialism. They did preserve as matters of common knowledge and common belief the common man's idea of himself: that he is a unique individual and uniquely valuable. If this idea persists as a commonplace of Christian doctrine, if Christianity persists as a commonplace profession, it is not due to the splendid writings, great speeches or heroic behaviour of one or more magnificent Christians—though such there were and such played their part—but to the widespread unheroic efforts of little men, little pastors, little sheep. There can be no rebellion without grounds of rebellion. It is the grounds of rebellion of which the little men have preserved the knowledge. There can be no rebellion except against wrong. It is the idea of right and wrong which the little ministers have kept alive" (*Belief*, p. 267).

All this did not arise from any doctrinaire democracy, any sentimental regard for "the masses", any invertedly snobbish contempt for learning and experience; the human perfectibility of man was a heresy that had no attraction for Gill, and his comments on "the suburbs" were exceeded in pungency only by his comments on workers' ambitions to emulate the suburbs. No. Just as man's chief means to culture, worship and the contemplation of being have from the beginning been the necessity of providing himself with food, clothing and shelter—ordinary things—so wisdom, knowledge and understanding derive and ramify from fundamental truths discernable, whether through reason or revelation, by the ordinary man, man the tool-using animal, such a man as Eric Gill. In England at the end of the nineteenth-century there were thousands of obscure families like the Brighton Gills; Eric's schooling was rather below the average in such families; he had no advantage of upbringing and the rest that he did not share with thousands of other young men; he was for years no more than a letter-cutter and stone-mason, living as such; when he found himself in a so-called superior environment for example, among artists and literary people, he did not like it and cleared out; he had no high and overmastering ambition; he was not endowed by nature with any abnormal intellectual ability, he read widely, but enthusiastically or critically rather than studiously: in a word, he was quite an ordinary man—but one who used to the utmost his mind, his will and his heart.

This is one of the reasons why Gill's criticism is so important. He was not like so many philosophers who argue from the abstract to the concrete without any practical experience of the concrete. In the order of time, Gill started with the concrete; like the carpenter in Miss Sackville-West's poem (I quote from memory and perhaps inaccurately), he knew what it was to "hold down Reality, struggling, to a bench": when he expounded a philosophy of work and art, it was, for once, a working artist speaking. He slowly worked from the concrete back to the abstract and, used to dealing with real things, he found that abstractions too are realities (in the measure of their truth)—and he handled them accordingly. It is sometimes necessary to screw a piece of wood tightly in a vice to keep it still: Gill found it is sometimes necessary metaphorically to screw an idea in a vice, for a similar reason and however impatient it may be of the treatment.

Eric lived for, worked for and spoke for and to his own kind. I have heard it said that, if he begins at the beginning, reads with attention and does not skip, any person of ordinary intelligence can understand the dozen volumes of St Thomas Aquinas's monumental *Summa*, but that no one without special training and knowledge can understand the works of Descartes and Comte, Kant and Berkeley. I have not attempted either exercise, so I do not know if this be true. But I do know that any simple fellow can read the writings of Eric Gill and find intelligible and convincing exposition of such daily and practical problems as God and man, matter and spirit, belief and science, personality, free will and responsibility, art, work and industry—all those things that are, whether we know it or not, of the first importance to every man jack of us. Gill wrote and spoke deliberately "on the level of ordinary human speech and thought", and so for the man Jack and the woman Jill, with no long words or technical jargon, no vague uplift or recondite notions, no metaphysical flights beyond the range of the kitchen and the bar (if only the kitchen and the bar would turn off the radio and pay attention thoughtfully for a bit): not these, but a straightforward examination of what are really everyman's problems, in language that everyman can understand, usually with illustrations that are at once familiar to him. And not only did Gill write what the ordinary person can read: he wrote what the ordinary person knows—but does not always know that he knows.

3

NICHOLAS BERDYAEV has said somewhere that Christian theology needs to be complemented by a Christian anthropology. He does not, I suppose, imply that there is no such thing, but that it needs to be studied more deeply and intensively and (especially in view of current theories and practice) brought before the people at large, non-Christian as well as Christian, with the earnestness and perseverance that has hitherto been reserved for theology. Eric Gill was in explicit agreement. His own most outstanding characteristic was integrality and completeness: he was a whole man, and every aspect of himself, his work and his beliefs, was integrated and interdependent, fused into one shining personality. He was a living and amazingly successful example of what he was always trying to do, what he called "my difficulty and my enthusiasm"—"to discover how things are related and to discover a right relation where a wrong one exists". It appeared to him that lack of integralness is *the* disease, the master disease, from which civilized mankind is suffering: we are not simply uprooted, we are torn to pieces.

The God of Christianity is the source of all being, Being itself, He Who Is, the God of Abraham, Isaac and Jacob. But this conception has been weakened and watered down till he is thought of merely as the Author of Nature or the Supreme Lawgiver or even—Heaven help us !—the Great Artificer who "made my mate": that is, if he is not simply the Unknown God. Just so with the Christian concept of man. He has been almost lost in a Heraclitan flux, become a creature who does, acts, becomes: "the doing is all." The concept of being has to be recovered also in relation to man. To-day it is no longer the personality of God alone that has to be upheld, but the personality of man as well. Each and every man and woman is an individual person to start with, who takes on communal functions; he is not a "functional unit which may or may not end up by developing individual idiosyncrasies". As an object of God's love his value is, as we say, absolute: he is an end, not a means. The state is a means to an end—man's good life and convenience: the Bible is a means, to the end that man may know and live the truth; Christ's resurrection was a means, to "our rebirth into the living hope". But man is, like the daisy in its eternal quality, or Dame Julian's nut, "a thing, a being in itself. It is not a means to an end. 'It lasteth and for ever shall, for God loveth it'." And it is not only in the face of such philosophies as fascism, nazism and communism that these things have to be maintained, that we have to uphold that man is "a creature who knows and wills and loves: a rational being, responsible for his acts and the intended consequences of his acts . . . made in the image of God (child of God and, if he will, heir also), a creature who loves" (*Machine Age*, p. 26).

Eric Gill based himself ultimately on man's consciousness; that consciousness testifies to his personality, and divine revelation enlarges and infinitely enriches that truth. And fundamental to the Christian idea of man is the further truth that he is made up of matter and spirit, both real and both good, manifestations of the same one reality, a figure of our theandric life with all its glories and trials that Eric constantly returned to. And in his thirst for right relations he never allows us to forget that "though there is a distinction of category between matter and mind, and though the mind is the ruling partner, the body and mind do not act separately. . . .

And so in man's history it is not possible to think that this or that was simply the product of environment, economic circumstance or material force, nor is it possible to think that such and such was simply the product of his spirit. The two parts or principles of man's being are inextricably intertwined and death for man is precisely the disintegration of matter and spirit" (*Belief*, p. 273).

Throughout Christian history there has been a tendency to belittle, or worse, the material side of human life, a tendency varying in strength from the formal heresies of encratic gnostics and manicheans, catharists and puritans, to the sometimes hardly less mischievous exaggerations of those orthodox people, of all denominations, who seek to keep themselves or others from sin, or to answer the question of evil, or to ensure a godly detachment from this world, by an attitude that seems to imply the essential evil of created matter, especially of the human body: so widespread and continuing is this manichean dualism (by no means confined to Christians) with its corollary of seeing asceticism as an end and not simply a means, that it looks as if it is a specific result of that spoiling of human nature that Christians call The Fall. Against it Gill struck hard and often, directly or indirectly, sometimes so regardlessly of contemporary convention that some were shocked to silence and others provoked to calling him names, from "pelagian" and "antinomian" to less "polite" expressions. But he went deeper than his critics, he saw the ultimate term of the false mysticism that would have us behave as pure spirits while yet inhabiting bodies: "The 'degradation' of making anything useful—the 'sordidness' of child-bearing—the 'mere animality' of digestion: such are the phrases of Sodom and Gomorrah. Such are the phrases of aesthetes, and they disclose the root ideas of puritanism. Matter is not good enough for man" (*Beauty*, p. 107). He was far from oblivious of the disorders that so properly alarm the moralist, but he did not trust for their remedy, humanly speaking, in mere negation, "Thou shalt not". God is the source of all enjoyment, and when we enjoy his creation in the way he intended we share his enjoyment.

"Adam could not see the Wood for the Tree. Adam sinned when he fell from contemplation (as the theologian says): that is to say when he saw himself as self-satisfactory, when, like Herod, 'he gave not God the honour'. There is indeed this danger. It is of course, and obviously, man's besetting sin. It is pride, the root of all sin. But the remedy is not the denial of enjoyment but the giving of thanks. The remedy is not the denial of material goods, but the recognition of material goods as gifts, and not only as gifts, but as gifts which signify the Giver" (*W. & L.*, p. 112).

And many of Gill's critics on this head failed to notice that, if he emphasized the goodness of material things strongly and often, he emphasized the primacy of spirit more strongly and more often. Sensual pleasures are called enthralling because they can make slaves of men, "and the worse slavery is the subjection of mind to matter, of the spiritual to the material, of the immeasurable to the measurable, of the infinite to the finite . . . Materialism spells slavery. Freedom, they say with one voice (Italian, German or Russian) 'freedom is a concession of the state'". Other tongues besides Italian, German and Russian go to make up that ghastly voice. Man is enslaved thus to-day to a terrifying degree, and this success of the materialist philosophers and propagandists has depended upon a monstrous suppression of truth, the truth about man's real nature and significance among created things.

"No religion has ever been such a 'dope'. Priests have endeavoured to make men think themselves worms before God. They have exploited men's sense of responsibility and their consequent sense of sin. But those who in their enthusiasm oppose religion have gone further still. Men are no longer worms before God. There is no God who could desire the death of a sinner. Man is of no importance to God, because he is of no importance at all. Man's appetite for abasement cannot be further exploited. However much Christian men have been taught to grovel before their Creator, they were at least taught as a dogma that God died for their redemption—they had that much intrinsic importance. The materialist does not grovel before his Creator; he just simply grovels, because grovelling is all he can do. He is a worm and no man. . . . We crawl on the face of the earth because our presence here has no other significance" (*Belief*, p. 150).

Nevertheless, materialism too is a philosophy—without a metaphysic, and a religion—without the infinite. The fact that more attention is paid in England to-day to banks and insurance-offices than to churches shows, not a loss, but a change of religion—ultimate reality is sought in material things rather than in things of the spirit; the productions of modern Europe are as much an index to dominant religious ideas as are those of the middle ages or of India; an aeroplane is no less the work and expresses the genius of a whole people than the cathedral at Chartres. And a decisive factor in riveting Gill's attention on Christianity in general and the Roman Catholic Church in particular was her age-long struggle against these two excesses, belief that the material life is all and belief that it is nothing; whatever the aberrations of some of her members and of unorthodox sects, she has been unwavering in her affirmation that matter and spirit are both real and both good, and that spirit has the primacy. Thus the Church rejects both Western materialism and Eastern idealism, and emerges as "the arbiter of East and West because she refuses the denials of either".

§

The principal connotation of the word "revolution" to-day is a drastic change in socio-economic organization and conditions; and Eric Gill's social principles can be summed up in these words: responsibility, poverty, love of God. On the last I need not dwell: if what I have already said does not persuade the reader that to Gill the one thing necessary is love of God and his Christ and a humble listening to the promptings of the Holy Spirit, then that reader must turn to Gill's own writings (as I hope he will in any case). Let him read the essay on art and holiness in *Work and Leisure*: I quote at random, from page 121: "Man is a creature who loves. Ultimately he can only love the holy. . . . Is the word 'holy' a stumbling-block (to the Jews a stumbling-block, to the Gentiles foolishness)? Why be afraid or shy of the word? Primarily it means hale and hearty, whole, unsullied, perfect and therefore of God—godly, sanctified, sacred; and therefore gay and light and sweet and cheerful and gracious. 'Oh taste and see how *gracious* the Lord is.' But gay—above all things gay. . . ."

Man has free will. "The freedom of the will, whether proved by argument or not, is a fact of human experience, and to be accepted as such. . . . Pathological states of mind apart—and let the psychologists enlarge the sphere of pathology as much as they can—the free will remains and man is master, captain of his soul." To have free will involves having responsibility, being responsible for what one chooses to do: "We know, we affirm, I know and I affirm that at the very core of our being, of my being, there is the fact of responsibility." Gill did not say much about freedom or liberty but was constantly referring to responsibility, and the one involves the other: responsibility cannot be used unless there be freedom. He quotes Aquinas: "The free man is responsible for himself, but for the slave another is responsible. . . . The highest manifestation of life consists in this: that a being governs its own actions. A thing which is always subject to the direction of another is somewhat of a dead thing. . . . Hence a man in so far as he is a slave is a veritable image of death." Christianity imperatively demands responsibility: profession of it must be freely chosen by a free act, it must be lived equally freely. The Church and slavery could not permanently co-exist, and this was a major factor in eventually bringing formal slavery to an end; where there is a diminished responsibility there Christianity cannot be fully developed or fully effective.

Gill was sometimes criticized for apparently making too sweeping generalizations about "the rich". The same objection can be (and has been) raised against many good Christians, such as St Basil and St John Chrysostom, and for that matter against the gospels themselves. In speaking of the hidden power of liturgical Latin, Gill says he does not believe that the words *Divites dimisit inanes* can in their English form, "The rich he hath sent empty away", convey "such a stupendously revolutionary threat as that which they do in fact convey". Obviously he did not take upon himself to make moral judgements on rich people, whether individually or collectively; he was concerned with what St Paul was concerned with, that revolutionary threat and the truth which lies behind it, which Gill stated in as forcible a half-dozen lines as he ever wrote: "There is no idolatry so destructive of charity, so desolating, there is nothing which so certainly obscures the face of God, as the desire of money—the root of all evil. 'The root of all evil!' Did I make up that phrase? No; it is the word of God to man. The root of all evil, the *root*. The root of all *evil*" (*Auto*., p. 194).

"The principle of poverty," he declared, "is the only one consonant with the nature and destiny of man and his material environment and condition." What is meant by this poverty? Not, of course, indigence, destitution, evil poverty; but good poverty, that spiritual thing, explicit in Christian teaching, which bears fruit in human life and works. "To go without, to give up, to lose rather than gain, to have little rather than much—that is its positive teaching. Blessed are the poor in spirit; the humble, the common man, the common woman, simple women, mothers of children—'How hard is it for a rich man to enter Heaven'. . . . But it is only in love that this poverty can be embraced" (*S. & S*., p. 56). "Is it not clear, beyond any possibility of doubt, that whatever other things may or must be said of the teaching of Christ and of the witness of his saints, it is the blessing of poverty which is the central fact of Christian sociology?" (*Machine Age*, p. 13). And our present organization, while it keeps many in dire want, insufficiency or grinding insecurity, holds up for our admiration and effort the pursuit of wealth and luxury; while many are ill-clad and ill-fed and ill-housed, many (and not only, or even principally, "the rich") have a standard of living that is absurdly high. It was this, the standard of living which the middle class and the emulators of the middle class consider their due, that specially outraged Eric's doctrine of poverty: when a trade-union might be expected to be discussing work it is found trying to shove or bolster up the standard of living, however much too high it may be already (see *Belief*, p. 61 *et seq*.).

If "money" is the ruling influence in the state, if production for profit rather than for use rules in industry, the fault is ultimately ours, because "money" is the ruling power in our hearts.

§

Responsibility is of two kinds. There is moral responsibility for what we do and intend or refrain from doing, and there is intellectual responsibility for the kind and quality of what we make, "make" being understood in no narrow sense. Gill constantly returned to the theme of how deeply the idea of "making" enters properly into man's life and informs his work (*cf.*, the popular "What has he *made* of his life?"). "Deeds done, when viewed in themselves and not simply as means to ends, are also to be regarded as things made."

Work, says the dictionary, is "the exertion of energy, physical and mental" otherwise than for purposes of recreation. God has made the world and man such that work is necessary for life and, since nothing that truly subserves our life can be bad, there can be no form of necessary work which is in itself degrading. Nevertheless, an idea is now very prevalent that physical labour is bad, a thing to be avoided so far as possible, though even in the most mechanized conditions there must be a basic element of such labour. In a Christian society there should be no kind whatever of physical work which is either derogatory to human beings or incapable of being ennobled and hallowed; therefore, said Gill, "at every turn our object must be to sanctify rather than to exclude physical labour, to honour it rather than to degrade it, to discover how to make it pleasant rather than onerous, a source of pride rather than of shame. . . . There is no kind of physical labour which is at one and the same time truly necessary to human life and necessarily either unduly onerous or unpleasant".

Our industrial civilization fosters and encourages the notion that much manual work is, of itself, sub-human drudgery; when the working life of thousands of factory "hands", shop-assistants, clerks, domestics, navvies and transport workers and labourers on our pitiful farms is considered, this seems to be true; and it appears obviously a good thing that, by the use of more machinery, more of this drudgery should be got rid of. Thus it has come about that people have come to believe that all physical labour is in itself bad. We seek to reduce it to a minimum and we look to our leisure time for all enjoyable exercise of our bodies. (The contradiction has been overlooked that if physical exercise be bad in work, then it is bad in play also.)

> "It should be obvious that it is not the physical labour which is bad but the proletarianism by which men and women have become simply 'hands', simple instruments for the making of money by those who own the means of production, distribution and exchange. And those who argue in favour of the still further elimination of physical labour on the ground that much manual labour is, of itself, sub-human drudgery are playing into the hands either of those for whose profit the mechanical organization of industry has been developed or of the communists and others who look to the 'leisure state' as the *summum bonum*. We must return again and again to the simple doctrine: physical work, manual labour, is *not* in itself bad. It is the necessary basis of all human production and, in the most strict sense of the words, physical labour directed to the production of things needed for human life is both honourable and holy."

Having through our cupidity and indolence degraded most forms of work, domestic and other, so that they are no longer to be viewed as pleasant, still less as sacred, having made men and women into "hands" and profit-making instruments, herded together in monstrous cities, "we turn round and curse the very idea of labour. To use the body, our arms and legs and backs, is now held to be derogatory to our human dignity. . . . It is at the very base of the Christian reform for which we stand that we return to the honouring of bodily work".

The contempt shown for manual work has not been extended to those activities which in modern times are distinguished as the "fine arts"; on the contrary, their practitioners are excessively honoured, and a kind of mythology or mystagogy has grown up which Eric Gill castigated under the name of "art nonsense": he devoted a whole book, *Art and a Changing Civilization*, to what he called "the debunking of art". The isolation of something called Art (with a big A), especially pictorial art and the aesthetic chatter that goes therewith, the putting of the artist on a pedestal as someone apart from and above other men, the cultivation of an absurd artificiality called the "artistic temperament", such things, he said, imply, "a bourgeois frame of mind, and are a notable product of a bourgeois society".

All the arts, whether "useful" or "fine", have their origin in man's fundamental needs, to supply himself with food, clothing and shelter, to pray to and praise God, to recreate himself; and accordingly Eric, putting aside all irrelevancies about emotion, self-expression, and the like, defined art simply by its earlier meaning, as "the well-making of what needs making", thus vastly extending its scope as commonly understood to-day. Time and again he quoted the words of Ananda Coomaraswamy: "An artist is not a special kind of man, but every man is a special kind of artist"; it was on the artist as workman, as a "collaborator with God in creating", that his thought on this matter was centred, the objective approach to work that was destroyed in so many arts by the Renaissance. "I would rather have brick-laying and turnip-hoeing done well and properly and high art go to the devil (if it must), than have high art flourishing and brick-laying and turnip-hoeing be the work of slaves" (*Auto.*, p. 177). It was again to the common man that he looked; his revolution was again away from the specialist, the expert, professionalism, towards the ordinary person and his needs.

> "I have no use at all for 'Art' as commonly understood to-day. . . . I would abolish the fine arts altogether. Music—let us sing in church and at work and at harvest-festivals and wedding parties and all such times and places. But let us abolish the concert-hall. Painting and sculpture—let us paint and carve our houses and churches and town-halls and places of business. But let us abolish art-galleries and royal academies and picture-dealers. Architecture—let us employ builders and engineers, and let them be imbued with human enthusiasms and not be moved merely by the desire for money or by merely utilitarian standards. Poetry—let those who can, write our hymns and songs and prayers. Let them write dirges for funerals and songs for weddings, and let them go about and sing to us or read to us in our houses. But let us abolish all this high nonsense about poets who are 'not as other men'. And let us abolish all the art-schools and museums and picture-galleries" (*W. & P.*, p. 87).

Fountain-pens, motor-cars and the like are as much works of art as pictures and carvings, the bridge across the Saint Lawrence river at Quebec would stand comparison with any medieval cathedral or castle; the difference between them is that the pictures and castles are the work of an individual artist—responsible workman—or a number of them working together, whereas the only artist concerned with the production of the motor-car or the bridge is the *designer*, architect, thereof, the others concerned being mostly willing or unwilling proletarian "hands". And each method faithfully reflects the philosophy and religion and life of a society: Chartres cathedral, simply as a building, could arise from none other than an ultimately spiritual background, the Canadian bridge is as clearly a product of the materialistic enthusiasms of the times in which we live.[1]

> "Work itself becomes a game, and the curse of Adam—'in the sweat of thy brow thou shalt eat bread'—is turned to blessing, for man has found joy in his labour and that that is his portion. Thus, while the necessity remains and use is neither denied nor condemned, all things made become works of love, all deeds become things in themselves, all means become ends. This is the basis, the concreted and untrembling foundation of human art. This is man's response to his responsibility—that he freely wills what is necessary, he makes what must be into a thing he has chosen.
>
> "These are the things which the materialism of our time denies and derides. By its separation of work from pleasure, its divorce of use from beauty and of beauty from meaning, it has produced a real disintegration of humanity, and on the basis of its materialism

[1] It may be noted in passing that Gill did not entertain the delusion that the culture of the past was Christian in the sense that it was in any way a direct product of the Church or of ecclesiastics. Medieval bishops, priests and monks were clergy and customers, not workmen and producers (with individual exceptions, of course). "In fact, the civilizing power of man is a lay power—fostered, encouraged, nursed, petted by the Church but, in its own sphere, independent. . . . [The Church] takes what she is given" (*Beauty*, p. 32). Strictly speaking, there is no such thing as a Christian or Catholic or Protestant culture: there are the various cultures which grow up in societies of people who are Catholics or Protestants or what not, which reflect the corresponding ideas more or less faithfully.

there is no remedy for its sufferings but a more efficient organization of material. Let there be plenty for all and no parasites. Let all the milk be sterilized. They say: Let thought be free and let all work be commanded. We say: There is no such thing as free thought and let all works be free offerings. Materialism spells slavery. . . . 'Freedom is a concession of the state'" (*Belief*, pp. 330–1).

And the ultimate slavery and degradation of the artist is to be "freed from the necessity of making anything useful".

4

SOME Christians made it a matter of reproach against Gill that *apparently* he did not pay enough attention to the cruelties and injustices of communists and their implacable persecution of all religion or to the cruelties and injustices of fascists and nazis and their subtle efforts to nullify the Church's influence.[1] They overlooked that in his writing and public speaking he was concerned more with diseases than with symptoms; and they were incredulous when assured that he did not believe that fundamentally and potentially the societies of Great Britain and the United States and France were much better than those of Russia and Italy and Germany; that, in effect, respectable "democratic" capitalist-industrialism is as atheistic, as destructive of responsibility and liberty, of holy poverty and the human person, of hope and love, as is communism itself; that its practical materialism has precisely the same effects as the dialectical materialism with which marxists oppose metaphysical and spiritual truth; that, in fact, totalitarian stateism, particularly in its communist form, is a logical development of the civilization of "the democracies".[2] No wonder communism seems the only just politics for the "beehive

[1] It is true that for a long time he held the view that militant godlessness is only an accident of marx-leninist communism, provoked by the insufficiency of and support of bourgeois exploitation by so many Christians. Later, I think, he came to realize that the destruction of spiritual religion is essential to marxist theory. In any case, it may be questioned whether stoning the prophets is worse than ignoring them altogether.

[2] He did not of course, as some fanatics do, claim that in the present war there is nothing to choose between the combatants. He saw many reasons why a victory for Great Britain and the United States and the defeat of the Axis powers offers hope for a desperate world, whereas the reverse would increase the desperation of our state. But that is little enough without a real "revolution".

state" that most people seem to want and few try to prevent, for if all things are to be made by machines within a "rationalized" system there must naturally be more and more standardization.[1]

Fascism and socialism and marxism do not offer holiness: they offer more physical convenience and psychological satisfaction (by flattering human sensibility) in return for the obedience of their citizenry. They tell us they are going to cure a disease—by aggravating it. "Had it not been for the spur which trade-unionism gave to human inventiveness and the consequent development of machinery it would very certainly have been necessary either to repeal the Factory Acts, and all acts designed to protect the animal classes, or else to abandon the ambition of being a first-class multiple-store and shopkeeping nation." The socialist movement "offered nothing in the way of divine inspiration, nothing beyond the ideal of a world in which all should be hygienically and warmly clad—with a sort of B.B.C. 'culture park' looming in the background; as though to say: When we've properly got going with the love of our fellow men, then we'll see what we can do about culture and, well, you know, religion and art and stuff" (*Auto.*, pp. 141, 163). The marxists go one worse. "They have thrown away the God whom the capitalists profess to worship and do not, and have accepted the servitude which capitalism has developed and perfected but whose existence the capitalists deny. Thus they have not emptied out the baby with the bath water. They have retained the bath water while emptying out the baby. They have emptied out the Baby of Bethlehem only to swallow the foul and befouling bath water of London and Manchester" (*Belief*, p. 271).

[1] But, like so large a number of people of very different views, Gill tended, I think, to exaggerate the popularity of communist views (even as vague aspirations) in England.

And not simply the slums and misery of those cities, which are accidental to our materialism (Are we not getting rid of them ?), but its substance—its philosophy, its reversal of human and spiritual values. If capitalism is as irreligious as socialism, socialism is as inhuman and enslaving as capitalism. For all its lip-service to the spirit, its church on Sundays, and museums and art-galleries and "Shakespeare for the workers", "business" is materialist. "For all their real devotion to pure art, pure science, or pure what-not, the reformers are as much materialists as the men of business. The communists among them are clearheaded enough to recognize this; they are honest enough to proclaim it and glory in it."

"Workers, throw off your chains !"—and then put them on again. No revolution that accepts materialism and its modern social incarnation, industrialism, can really be a revolution.

It was, then, central to the social-revolutionary aspect of Eric Gill's teaching that industrial capitalism implies a way of life and work that is inconsistent with man's nature and with the Christian religion. Capitalism is a social theory based on the profit-motive, and its essence and object is production for profit; both "labour" and "products" must be looked at primarily from the point of view of saleability, and not from that of their intrinsic quality and man's real needs. Its method is that of industrialism, which had three main processes, viz., the proletarianization of the craftsman, of the agricultural worker, and of the "small man" generally, the concentration of production in factories, and the use of machines, leading to mass-production by the division and subdivision of labour.

"Eric Gill," wrote Father Kenelm Foster, O.P., "holds things together. He is our great *pontifex*, bridge-builder.

Spirit and matter, body and mind, knowing and loving: he distinguished them with exquisite clarity, and then held them together. He did it *in practice;* wherever he went he made matter alive with rational beauty. Why did he loathe industrialism?—fundamentally because he thought that *in practice* it separates what God has joined together, the body and the mind." That was indeed the main point among his many serious charges against industrialism: not its cruelty (for it is now realized that too obvious unkindness "does not pay"), but "the change which it has brought about in the nature of the work to be done and therefore in the minds of the men who do it"; it produces a world wherein "on the one hand we have the artist concerned solely to express himself; on the other is the workman deprived of any self to express". He did not assert that this was anything new in the world's history: the attempt to divorce art from work and use from beauty has been made—and resisted—from the beginning. But industrialism leads so clearly to the separation of mind and matter, which spells death to man, that death may be said to be its very object.

"It is only as persons that we serve one another, and when personal control is divorced from ownership it is only with great difficulty that men retain responsibility for the form and quality of what is done or produced . . . the men have no responsibility whatever, except a moral responsibility to obey the terms of their contract, *i.e.*, to do what they are told. Thus the craftsman is finally degraded—he ceases to be a person who in any way designs what he makes and makes what he designs; he is no longer even a hand: he has become a tool, a sentient part of the machine" (*Machine Age*, pp. 34, 38)—and this without overlooking the real love of machines and the great skill and craftsmanship displayed both by machine-makers and machine-minders. "Our industrial system does not enslave the workers in any legal or technical or political sense. It does not necessarily maltreat their bodies or coerce their minds. It simply reduces the workman to a subhuman condition of intellectual irresponsibility.[1] It simply separates, divorces, the material and the spiritual." More and more workmen are being deprived of intellectual responsibility, becoming automatons in their work, prevented from being artists.

> "And in their leisure, the time when they are not working they must be content to be amused; for industrialism has deprived them of the necessity of making anything useful." "The value of the creative faculty derives from the fact that that faculty is the primary mark of man. To deprive man of its exercise is to reduce him to subhumanity. . . . A man is as out of place in a factory as in a lightless dungeon. . . . If the populations of our factory-towns were not constantly recruited from the country they would wither intellectually as certainly as they wither morally and physically" (*W. & P.*, pp. 84–85).

Intellectual responsibility the concern of a few, or one; for the rest, obedience: the idea has become painfully familiar in other spheres besides industry.

It is more horrible, wrote Gill, that men of business should rule us through the profit-making system they have perfected, and impose their foul view on the world, "than it would be if the whole race of men and women should rot their bodies with lechery and drunkenness". It produces things which, in their nature, because of the manner of their production, are unsuitable for the use of human beings: "We are making a bee-hive when we should have a house. We are making an apiary when we should have a motherland." The thing and its results

[1] Gill quoted this aphorism so often that he made it his own. It originated, I believe, with Father Martin d'Arcy. S.J.

have been summed up in words that might have been spoken by Eric Gill but, in fact, came from Pope Pius XII: "In this age of mechanization the human person becomes merely a more perfect tool in industrial production and . . . a perfected tool for mechanized warfare."

Eric did not deny the impressiveness of the powers which industrialism has helped to confer on us, or seek to decry them. He had no romantic ideas about the "immorality" of using machinery, nor did he suppose its use was likely to be noticeably lessened in any foreseeable future. "It is art-nonsense to say that because the Forth Bridge is made of iron it is not a work of art. . . . It is no more immoral to make things by machinery than by hand. It is immoral to make things badly and pretend that they are good, and no amount of 'hand' is an excuse for stupidity or inefficiency" (*Art Nonsense*, pp. 313–14). The trouble is that machines are not simply complicated tools designed by workmen to help them in their work. "They are things designed to enable their owners to make things in great quantities in order to make great quantities of money. No definition of machinery and no description of machine industry can neglect these facts. . . . The real distinction between tools and machines is discovered in the sphere of control and responsibility. Who is responsible for the thing made or the deed done?" (*Belief*, pp. 103, 88).

It was characteristic of his all-roundness and freedom from "teetotalism" that Gill was interested in machines (*e.g.*, the internal-combustion engines of the lorries he drove in the R.A.F.) and appreciative of their beauty—so like the beauty of bones and crystals and insects' wings; I have seen him stand entranced before a shop-window full of useful gadgets and neatly-fitting boxes and files. It was not for nothing that for ten youthful years he drew nothing but locomotive engines, held by the "character and meaning that were manifest in their shape". Need it be said there is no inconsistency here? On one occasion, asked by the proud owner of a sham-gothic residence how he liked the building, Eric replied that he liked the electrical switchboard in the hall. His questioner expressed surprise. "Oh, I like anything reasonable," explained Eric, to which his host replied, "That's too abstruse for me." When it is added that the owner was a scientist that anecdote becomes even more significant.

§

Eric Gill's indictment of industrialism has been widely misunderstood, and his sweeping generalizations of its evil effects sometimes gave understandable offence. When he said time and again that it reduces the workers to a subhuman condition of intellectual irresponsibility, the word "intellectual" was not always heard; when he said so often that the industrial population is dehumanized he did not always add that he meant dehumanized as workmen, as makers of things: machine-minding is often very skilful work and many mechanics are highly skilled and responsible workmen, but they are so in relation to the machine and not to the thing which the machine turns out. It would have been well had he more frequently and clearly stated his recognition of "the many men, and women, who in spite of the inhuman nature of their employment, retain the notions which properly belong to private and personal enterprise" (*Machine Age*, p. 35). Even so, from our own personal experience of people, we may think that he exaggerated, and in respect to present actuality perhaps he did: but he was looking also to the future—and he was a far-seeing man.

Again, when in answer to the oft-made objection that "A man can be a good Christian in a factory", he replied,

"Yes; and St Agnes was a good Christian in a brothel —but that was no reason why she should stay there!" it is not surprising that the objector should not be silenced, for the analogy between a factory and a brothel does not go very far. Of course he knew perfectly well, he never forgot, that Christianity can enable us to lead godly, righteous and sober lives amid any conditions: his point was that some conditions are more favourable than others. "A social order cannot in itself force any one to do anything, but it can be such as to place many obstacles in the way" of those who would live in a human and Christian manner: in a score of places (*e.g.*, *Art Nonsense*, p. 132), he sets out briefly, clearly and cogently why the conditions of industrialism are so bad in this respect, and it is only common prudence to remove removable handicaps. His case is most forcibly and brilliantly set out in *Money and Morals*, but its presentation there also showed most manifestly an element of exaggeration. It is gravely false, it is shocking, to say that "It is waste of time teaching Christian morals in the present condition of things", as he himself at once goes on to admit; but his admission is too reserved. It is true that the exercise of heroic virtue can't be counted on—but the grace of God can. He is on surer ground when he declares that "truth and error cannot permanently lie down together and Christian morals cannot *permanently flourish* in the same bed with a life contrary to nature" (*italics mine*).

That just as right thinking precedes right faith, so a certain way of living is the necessary preamble to Christian morals, is quite true if rightly understood; but it can be distorted, and it is easy to overlook that if Eric set that "certain way of living" very high it was because he was also looking at a very high and enlightened and unrestricted standard of life and conduct. And why should

F

he not? Are we not bound to? "Be ye perfect. . . ." Moreover, on the psychological side, there was the factor of reaction. In his dealings with his fellow Christians he was met on all sides by clergy, the shepherds of the flock, who seemed to seek every excuse to avoid finding fault with industrial capitalism: among Catholics, in spite of the outspoken social encyclical-letters of Pope Leo XIII and Pope Pius XI, he did not find "clergy and laity all agog for social or any other reform, and in general the clergy seem to regard it as their job to support a social order which, so far as it is possible, forces us to commit all the sins they denounce" (*Auto.*, p. 214). What seemed to him so unbelievable, shocking and blasphemous was the complacency of apparently the majority of Christians, not only about the purity of their faith and practice, but also about the *kind* of world in which they live and which they have co-operated in making.

In any case, it seemed to Gill, the Christians who ask the question, "Is communism (or capitalism or nazism or what-not) compatible with Christianity?" are approaching the matter from the wrong end. The proper question is, "Is Christianity compatible with the industrial and authoritarian development of society?" And the answer is certainly, "No": for at the root of Christianity is the doctrine of individual personal responsibility. "Man is man all the time, and not only in his spare time."

In *The Problem of Pain* C. S. Lewis has given us a timely warning against "making use of the idea of corporate guilt to distract our attention from those humdrum, old-fashioned guilts of our own which have nothing to do with 'the system' and which can be dealt with without waiting for the millenium." In *Christianity and Crisis* Reinhold Niebuhr writes: "We do not find it particularly impressive to celebrate one's sensitive conscience by enlarging upon all the well-known evils of our Western world and equating them with the evils of the totalitarian systems." Substituting "capitalist-industrial" for "totalitarian" in the second quotation, no one who knew him or attentively reads his writings will imagine for a moment that Eric Gill stood in need of such warnings: but they do indicate very real dangers for those of us who share his thought. He was a man of peculiarly well-balanced mind and sensitive conscience, and all those of us who would follow him are not similarly well equipped: it was said by a friend precisely of Gill and a third party that "God sends disciples to geniuses to keep them humble". It is not given to everyone who sees the evils and abuses of industrial capitalism to see them in their setting so clearly or to examine them and their possible remedies with such precision as did Eric Gill; and very few of us are enabled more or less to escape them (though we shall be wise to do so if we get the chance, as St Benedict escaped from the evils of sixth-century Rome).[1] But we can safely and surely do what Eric writes of so movingly and delicately in quite another context on pages 223–27 of the *Autobiography*, we can take the delights and dangers and evils of the society in which we live and, following the words of that same St Benedict in the prologue to his *Rule*, "cast them on the rock which is Christ".

In face of industrialism, as of every other similar question, we have to beware of the exaggeration contrary to the excessively moralistic interpretation of Christianity: it must not be obscured that the Christian religion has directly to do with only two problems—sin and virtue. It can be applied to ploughing up pasture or to poetry only through being effectively applied to the problem of

[1] Eric defined the chief aim of his life's work to be "to make a cell of good living in the chaos of our world"; to do something towards "reintegrating bed and board, the small farm and the workshop, the home and the school, the earth and Heaven".

sin and virtue in farmers and poets. It can be applied to society only through the individual members of society: the disappearance of industrial capitalism, the establishment of one of these "Christian orders" we hear so much about, could by themselves effect little for the kingdom of God. "The holiness of God is something more and other than moral perfection"—but without moral goodness there can be no holiness at all, no wholeness. Eric Gill tried to live in the light of "Seek first the kingdom of God, and his righteousness"[1] and, as has been said before, he more and more found the way to that kingdom to be through the word of St James, "pure religion and undefiled is this, to visit the fatherless and widows in their affiiction and to keep unspotted from the world".

§

"No individual Christian in our society is to be condemned except in so far as he approves or promotes the evil thing. And, again, no individual, in relation to our society, is to be praised except in so far as he promotes the Christian revolution (*i.e.*, 'turning round') by which once more a Christian society may be revived" (*W. & P.*, p. 6). In his article in *Blackfriars* already referred to, Bernard Kelly remarks that: "The categories in which Gill lived, worked, and wrote were absolute: religious, moral, metaphysical. They were not the categories of political expediency. Thus he was eminently qualified in the critique of social programmes, Catholic and not, put forward to restore a tolerably Christian social structure, but he was not qualified to judge them precisely as

[1] In reading Gill it must be borne in mind that the Rheims-Douay version of the Bible translates δικαιοσύνη, *iustitia*, not by "righteousness" but "justice". This is rather misleading, since in current use the connotation of the word "justice" is almost entirely rational and juridical.

politically feasible." Or, as Eric put it, politics are not my line of business; if he agreed with the Reverend F. H. Drinkwater that "the economic problem fills the whole sky", yet the only socio-economic reform he put forward (apart from his insistence on production for use and not for profit, and with one notable exception to be mentioned later) was the abolition of the middleman and the financier.

Way back as an architect's pupil in London he had realized that "it was not so much the working *class* that concerned me as the working man—not so much what he *got* from working as what he *did* by working", and had got hold of the notion that "a good life wasn't only a matter of good politics and good buildings and well-ordered towns and justice in economic relations". Social reform is the business of those who know the nature and destiny of man, he declared, and "the trouble with the present age is that it is just the knowledge of those things which it is most uncertain about, and consequently politics and social guidance are left to a crowd of amateurs—novelists, multiple-storekeepers, manufacturers of motor-cars or chemicals—whose profession of disinterestedness is only slightly more credible than that of thieves and robbers" (*Art Nonsense*, p. 315); and in the first essay of *Work and Property* he conveniently summarized some of the things that these amateurs ought to know.

As for the professional politicians—"Liberals and Conservatives—Labour! All these parties wish to preserve the *status quo*. But it is just the *status quo* which is in question." People of all kinds toy with communism both because it seems better politics than *that* and because it seems to offer an approximation to absolutes in a world wherein religion has grown cold: afraid to face Love, too tired to rebuild his house, they "fall back on an 'economic interpretation of history', and are satisfied to live by bread alone". It was in Palestine that Gill fully realized in all their beastliness the materialism, exploiting imperialism and mechanized labour in which England has been a pathfinder and pioneer, and he came back determined to keep clear of all politics and politicians.

> "For . . . politics is beyond me. Politics is . . . outside my scope, something I can't do. Moreover I do not believe political arrangements and rearrangements are real. It is all a confused business of ramps and rackets—pretended quarrels and dishonest schemings, having no relation to the real interests of peoples. . . . The prestige of Parliament is an empty fraud. It is not too much to say that [parliamentarians] are not and never have been anything but agents for the defence of monetary interests. Such was the origin of parliamentary representation, such is its very soul. . . . And, particularly, do not believe politicians. By the nature of their trade they have no professional pride and can have none. The phrase 'professional politician' has brought the very notion of professionalism to dirt" (*Auto.*, pp. 259, 148).

Again there is an element of exaggeration, but it would be pharisaical to stress it. Years before Eric had been strongly impressed by Julien Benda's book, *La Trahison des Clercs* (called in the English version *The Great Betrayal*); he came to see even more clearly that the poet, the artist, the scholar, the "clerk", who should be a disinterested[1] man, is indeed a traitor if he puts himself almost unreservedly at the service of the relative and contingent: and if it be a question of professional

[1] In view of an increasing misuse of this word it seems desirable to point out that it is *not* a synonym for "uninterested". I think Eric himself defined the saint as "the wholly disinterested man".

politics, he will be buried under a mountain of mud, "whereas it is necessary that he should keep his feet on the earth and his head above ground". In the words of The Preacher, without the craftsmen and the husbandmen the city cannot be built or flourish, "but they shall not dwell or go up and down therein; nor shall they go up into the assembly or sit among the judges". In other words, let them keep out of politics. "Nevertheless they shall strengthen the state of the world, and their prayer shall be in the work of their craft. . . ."

The increasing "politicization" of people in these latter days was very grievous to Gill; for himself he hardly ever adverted of his own accord to such concepts as democracy, dictatorship and the like. A man who was about to address a meeting of war-resisters asked him for a message to them. "Tell them to keep clear of politics," was the reply.

Politics even at its best is quite insignificant beside Christian doctrine and its implications. The "Magnificat" is irrelevant in our dirty struggles between "interests" and classes and nations and political programmes—so it must be the struggles themselves that are really irrelevant. "Religion is politics, and politics is brotherhood," said William Blake—"and brotherhood is poverty," added Eric Gill.

> "All our politics," he wrote in a publication of the Cotswold Bruderhof, "are based on a denial of the Gospels. Our capitalist society is founded solely upon the notion that those who have money have the duty to get more, and that those who have none must be enslaved or exploited or 'employed'—until machines make their existence unnecessary. The fascist societies want to create empires and become as rich and great as the others. The communist societies want to make the rich poor in order that the poor may become rich.

But the Church of God wants to make the rich poor and the poor holy.

"This is the circle of human politics: When we have accepted poverty there will be peace among men. Only when we make peace shall we become the children of God. Only when we love God shall we love our fellow men. Only when we love our fellow men shall we have peace. When we have peace we shall have poverty, and when we have poverty we shall have the kingdom of Heaven."

§

Remembering that by poverty Gill meant, where material goods are concerned, not less than a reasonable sufficiency for decent human life, it need occasion no surprise that he saw the chief "practical" means to the restoration of the dignity of physical work, and of the quality of things made, in the ownership of property; and he came to advocate as a practicable necessary reform the ownership of the means of production by the workers (*not* by the state; "workers" means all who work in a given enterprise, including the managing director if he works and if there is a job for him to do). This can be found set out in the essay on Work and Property in the book of that name and in another, "Ownership and Industrialism", in *Sacred and Secular;* but here I follow mainly a letter to the *Catholic Herald* newspaper in which he summarized his argument.

The right to property, he said, is not primarily a moral right, one due to man on account of his free will, but is, so to say, an intellectual right, due on account of his intelligence: it follows from man's material necessities and intellectual nature, deriving not from his need to *use* things but from his need to *make* things. As a moral being purely as such, man has no right of private ownership; he quotes Pope Leo XIII and Aquinas on the duty to possess things not as one's own but as common. (Incidentally, Christians, especially the Catholic clergy, have made a big mistake in presenting the right to private property as apparently simply a matter of morals, "a thing good men believe in and bad men deny, and that's all about it". We have sought to defend the institution of private property by the very arguments which are our opponents' strongest line of attack: "the earth is the Lord's", his gift to us is for our "individual appropriation and public use"—and we have done our best to destroy both, and so allowed such miseries to be heaped upon man that the socialist says, "Destroy private property!" to which the communist adds, "And religion with it!", for it has been made to look as if the Church herself were on the side of big business and exploitation.)

It is, then, to man as workman, as an intelligent being who must manipulate things in order to make them serviceable, that private ownership is both necessary and a natural right, and only when there is full control of the means of production can there be proper and efficient manipulation. Unless the farmer own the fields (or have a tenancy on terms nearly equivalent to ownership) he cannot exercise his best skill and intelligence upon them; unless the carver own the tools and stone he cannot properly exercise his skill and intelligence therewith; unless the miner own the mine, individually or jointly with others, he or they cannot properly control the job of mining. This necessity of manipulation it is which gives the right of private property in the means of production: "The exercise of art or work, whether it be that of a craftsman or a manual labourer, is the formal reason of individual appropriation", as Maritain observes.

It is obvious that, as things are, the ground upon which alone a claim to private property in productive goods can be validly made has to a considerable extent been destroyed. The factory "hand" can make no claim to private ownership in his work and the big-machine industries and transport are no longer in any true sense private enterprises: they are (as their directors boast) public services. Hence the moral force of communism: what are public services should be publicly owned for the profit of all. There no longer remains any rational and Christian objection to communal ownership, since the only reason for private ownership, the intellectual operation of the workman by which he imprints on matter the mark of rational being, has been destroyed by the development of machine industry.

The conclusion is inescapable. We cannot have any right to private property in the means of production unless we are prepared to abandon industrialism; most people are not so prepared, and even if they were, it would be impossible to return immediately to pre-industrial methods.

> "Let us resolutely put away all dreams of that sort. Let us abandon the coteries of vegetarians and nut-eaters and artist-craftsmen. . . . Politics deals with things as they are. . . . Ownership is necessary to human happiness, to human dignity and virtue, and ownership means control. A share in profits is not ownership. Money in the savings-bank is not control of the means of production. The only desirable and at the same time the only possible reform of 'our world' is distribution of ownership" (*S. & S.*, p. 168).

Capitalist organization implicitly and communist organization explicitly lead to public ownership for private use. This is the exact opposite of Christian society, where there should be private ownership for the sake of common use. In our existing society we have degraded nearly all production and transport to being huge impersonal and therefore subhuman enterprises—and yet we have the insolence or folly to endeavour to maintain private ownership in the use of productive things and to declare that this sort of "private property" is a principle of Christianity which must be defended against ravening "reds" and subversive "leftists". "The newspapers and politicians and big-businessmen talk as though everybody in England had private property, and enough private property to make complete human beings of themselves, and as though it was only in wicked Russia that no one was allowed to own anything privately" (*Unemployment*, p. 27).

Workers' ownership of the means of production, then, was what Gill put forward as a practicable, perhaps the only practicable, step towards the Christian society in which there shall be private ownership for the sake of public use, a private ownership not asked for "on the selfish ground of private enjoyment, but for the sake of the good of things to be made and in order that the public use which morality demands may be a use of good things". The alternative we shall have to accept is in all probability some form of communistic industrialism and the "leisure state", wherein man's intelligence will wither away in highbrow snobbery or mob vulgarity.

> But "that alternative is no revolution, it is simply *progress*. In fact so-called revolutionaries are simply 'progressives'. They want, instead of the present world, the world which the present one *implies*. They want the same thing only more so—the same things only more of them. . . . Merely to transfer ownership from private persons to the state is no revolution; it is only a natural development. Government by the proletariat is no revolution; it is only the natural sequel to the enfranchisement of lodgers. But to abolish the

proletariat and make all men owners—and to abolish mass-production and return to a state of affairs wherein 'the artist is not a special kind of man but every man is a special kind of artist'—that would be a revolution in the proper sense of the word. And merely to proclaim an atheist government is no revolution—for that would be to make explicit what is already implicit in capitalist commercialism; but to return to Christianity would be truly revolutionary" (*W. & P.*, pp. 53–54).

§

Meanwhile—let us lift up our hearts to the Lord.

"I am quite perfectly certain that the ultimate truth of the created universe is that which is implied in the saying of Julian of Norwich: 'It lasteth and forever shall, for God loveth it', and that as the actuality of everything is dependent upon God's will, so everything is sustained in being by his love."

In that belief Eric Gill lived, and in that belief he died.

www.ingramcontent.com/pod-product-compliance
Lightning Source LLC
LaVergne TN
LVHW020652100826
845148LV00012B/2457

* 9 7 8 1 5 3 2 6 8 4 7 7 7 *